THE COMPLETE GUIDE TO

GHOSTWRITING

THE COMPLETE GUIDE TO GHOSTWRITING

TEENA LYONS

THISTLE
PUBLISHING

This edition first published in 2014 by:

Thistle Publishing
36 Great Smith Street
London
SW1P 3BU

www.thistlepublishing.co.uk

ISBN-13: 978-1-910198-64-3

To
Anton, Julian and Woody

ABOUT THE AUTHOR

Teena Lyons spent ten years as a news reporter and feature writer on national newspapers and consumer magazines including Mail on Sunday, The Guardian, Sunday Times and Cosmopolitan before leaving Fleet Street in May 2006 to pursue a career as a ghostwriter. Teena has ghosted more than twenty books, ranging from biographies, to 'how to' style business books, to misery memoirs.

For more information on Teena Lyons, please see her website at www.professionalghost.com

ACKNOWLEDGEMENTS

This book would not have been possible without the kind help of the many people in the publishing industry who agreed to be interviewed and tell me about their experiences. Many ghosts, editors, agents and publishers spoke to me on condition of anonymity. I am, however enormously grateful to everyone, named or unnamed, who gave up their time to give invaluable insight into what it takes to make a great ghosting collaboration.

I would also like to thank my agent Andrew Lownie, in particular. He was very encouraging when I first went to him with the idea and has provided sage advice throughout. Thank you too to David Haviland at Thistle for overseeing the publication.

Heartfelt thanks should also go out to all the people I have ghosted for over the years. Each person has taught me so much about subjects I may sometimes have previously known nothing about and I have enjoyed every single project I have collaborated on.

Finally, thank you to my husband Anton and two boys Julian and Woody, who have always believed in this ghost.

INTRODUCTION
GHOST WRITING - (ONE OF) THE OLDEST PROFESSIONS

Ghostwriting is not a new profession. For centuries well-off people have sought out the services of a decent scribe who is content to pen their tale for financial reward. Arguably it all began with the Bible, which writers fashioned over time from oral recitation, although they wouldn't have called themselves ghostwriters. Since then, ghosts have brought us some of our best-known works and much ink has been wasted on speculating which famous historic writers may or may not have relied on the occasional help from an invisible hand (we're looking at you Misters Shakespeare, Dumas and Homer).

It's thanks to the help of ghosts that fans of more modern writers are able to buy new works long after the originator has shuffled off to the great library in the sky. Even living bestselling authors have trusted their brand to ghosts. Tom Clancy, for example, credits 'co authors' on his more recent thrillers, while James Patterson, who constantly has books in the bestseller lists, also admits to working with other writers so he can keep up with his prolific publishing schedule. Established authors pass their trusted collaborators a detailed outline of a new novel and then leave them to flesh it out while they presumably go off to think about other great storylines.

The modern boom in ghosting can, in part, be traced back to various publishing phenomena in the last century. In the early 1900s, for example, the majority of books read by American children were apparently written by one man; Edward Stratemeyer. Stratemeyer entranced an entire generation with dozens of mystery stories that opened up a new world of excitement and adventure. Demand was so great, the author developed more and more mystery series and new characters. Among these new characters were the *Hardy Boys* and *Nancy Drew,* who played starring roles in some of the most well loved children's books of all time. Stratmeyer wrote many of the series under a pseudonym, so as not to dilute his brand and so he could deal with several different publishers at the same time. The trouble was, it was tough to churn out enough books to satisfy the appetite for more books that was coming at him from all sides. So what did he do? Hire ghostwriters of course. He ensured they all kept to a strict, tried and tested, formula. Under his rules each and every chapter had to end with a cliff-hanger, plus each book would begin with a recap of the previous book and a preview of the next one. He'd send a ghost a synopsis of the book he wanted and a manuscript would be sent back several months later. The formula developed over time and it was pure publishing gold.

Hundreds of books were produced under Stratemeyer's system and he dominated the market. No one was any the wiser of his unseen helpers, or indeed just how prolific he had been, until a trial in the late 1970s over the question of copyright to the *Nancy Drew* and *Hardy Boys* books.

This assembly line model is not unique to Stratemeyer. The *Goosebumps* series for children by R. L. Stine had such a good response from publishers and readers the author had to turn to ghosts in later life to produce sequels.

Today, the demand for ghostwriters is being fuelled, at least in part, by an appetite for books authored by celebrities whose name alone will virtually guarantee sales. Such books are to publishing what Bruce Willis or Robert De Niro vehicles are to cinema. They might not be a sure thing, but they are as close to it as it is possible to get. Although it would be an over-exaggeration to say nearly every book written by a celebrity or politician is ghosted by a professional writer, a large majority are.

The list of celebrity tell-alls is long and studded with stars, from actors, to politicians, to musicians, to captains of industry. They have the story and they need a story teller. Most are unafraid to reach out for help too. They accept they are either too busy, or not experienced enough to turn out an entire manuscript by themselves and the answer is to bring in an expert.

It's quite likely that *at least* 50 per cent or more books in some genres have some sort of ghosting involvement. Indeed, some publishers say that as many as 7 out of 10 of their books are ghosted. It's not just A-listers who are getting ghostwritten nowadays either. While the bestseller lists are full of celebrity memoirs, these books now jostle with leadership biographies, political diaries and real life stories from ordinary people who have lived extraordinary lives.

Ghosts help satisfy an appetite among book buyers to read the true, in depth, stories of previously unknown people who have lived through remarkable events. Take, as just one example, the incident in January 2009, when a geese strike disabled the engines of a US Airways Flight, forcing captain Chesley 'Sully' Sullenberger to perform a heroic emergency landing on the Hudson River, a hair's breadth from downtown Manhattan. World media attention was focussed on the seemingly impossible smooth landing. Dramatic pictures of passengers and crew waiting on the plane's wings framed by the Manhattan skyline whetted the public appetite to find out more about the pilot. Sure enough, nine months later, Sullenberger's biography *Highest Duty: My Search for What Really Matters* hit the bookshelves. How did the pilot, who also worked as a crash investigator and CEO of a safety management consultancy find time to pen his story? With the help of an able literary co pilot, or ghost, as we know them. In Sullenberger's case, he worked with journalist and author Jeffrey Zaslow. The giveaway is the credit below the pilot's name saying: *with* Jeffrey Zaslow.

Rapid technological changes in the publishing world have further opened up the concept of ghosting to 'ordinary' people. Real life stories don't just have to be about fearless pilots who have saved dozens of lives. They could be stories of triumph over the most unbelievable odds, survival, or pretty much any inspiring tale. There is a demand among readers to buy these books and it is now easier for ordinary people to take a punt and write them. The cost of producing books has decreased substantially, thanks to digital and print on demand, plus the presence of easy-to-access marketplaces like Amazon make it easier for potential readers to find and buy books, without them having to be mass produced and distributed to bookshops around the country. In short, it is now much easier for new entrants to publishing and the number of books published by small independent presses, or even simply self published by the author themselves, has increased exponentially. The barriers to entry for people wanting to share their memoires are nothing like as onerous as they were even just a few years ago.

This democratisation of story-telling has opened up a new world for ghostwriters and the numbers in their ranks have swelled considerably. The increase in the quantity of books coming out corresponds with the growth in demand for professional authors to help write those books in the most compelling manner possible.

Let's not forget the reader's role in this either. The relationship between book buyer and book writer has changed irrevocably in recent years. It wasn't that long ago that reading books was sold to us as some sort of self improvement activity, part of some upwardly mobile longing. Great writing was sought out to improve the character and as part of a continuous stimulation programme for our grey matter. Although reading books would entertain, the activity would educate too. The popularity of the supermarket paperback proves that lofty ideal has been completely eroded. Book buyers who pop a copy of the celebrity 'tell all' into their trolley beside their tinned tomatoes, want to be entertained. To hell with improving the soul. When the twenty-some-thing, winning contestant of the latest round of Big Brother pens his or her life story it is not to satisfy demand to know more about their motivations and philosophies. It is because the public want to know what it is like to sleep with this contestant or that and how much alcohol was consumed in the making of the show. The 'celebrity' has nothing else of value to say. In this environment, specialist co writers are a necessary evil to pick the stories that will elevate the author in a reader's mind, by emphasising the scandalous, picking out the most shocking and nodding at the unusual. Today, what a person has done is much more interesting than what they've written.

To get an idea of how widespread ghosting now is, pull out a dozen copies of any non fiction book or autobiography from your own book shelf. The chances are a significant percentage will be written 'with' a ghost. And that is just the books that prominently acknowledge a co writer. Many give a far more subtle nod to the help of a professional, while some do their best not to mention it at all. Puzzling out the often vague reference to Mr or Ms X for their 'literary help', or for 'blending their thoughts with mine' is something of an obsession for those in the industry and there are some real treasures. US comedian and actor Tim Allen, for example, thanks David Rensin who collaborated on his bestseller *Don't Stand Too Close to a Naked Man*: 'Together we sought truth, enlightenment and the quantum punch line. He was good company.'

Some named authors will vehemently deny the aid of ghosts and will go as far as to go on prime time TV to relate elaborate stories of their writing routines to 'prove' they are the actual author of their books. John F Kennedy went to his grave denying that his Pulitzer-Prize winning Profiles in Courage was written by speechwriter Ted Sorensen, only for Sorensen's involvement to be revealed four decades later. Similar claims regularly pop up about other bestselling authors, but the chances are, we'll just never know in our lifetime. At the other end of the scale, there are people such as actress and singer Kerry Katona who freely admit to using ghosts and then go one stage further by saying they have never actually read books published under their own name.

Ironically, the boom in ghosting has fuelled a genre of celebrity ghosts, where the co writer's name is no longer a well kept secret. These ghosts can command top dollar to be involved in a collaboration. In the UK, ghosts such as Andrew Crofts, Pepsi Denning, Fanny Blake and Lynne Barrett-Lee are in demand while, across the Atlantic, a big name such as William Novak has gone from a fee of $80,000 for his first project *Iacocca*, penned in 1984, to commanding multi-million dollar advances. The reason they can command high fees is because it is seen as a badge of honour to get them in on a project. It can even form part of the marketing strategy because it demonstrates a book's good quality. Ghosting has become a selling point. Indeed, in a fantastic twist, in some cases it is *the* central marketing message. In the early Nineties, when Newsweek journalist Joe Klein penned Primary Colors, about Bill Clinton's first presidential campaign, he knew his book stood a better chance of success if it had a celebrity name on the front cover. That wasn't an option, so he ghost wrote his own novel and credited it to the fantastically intriguing 'Anonymous'.

In recent years, ghosting has become accepted as a division of mainstream writing. Writers can be authors, journalists, marketeers or ghosts. There are many categories and genres of ghost too, with some specialising in sporting biographies, others showing expertise at misery lit and some who get the pick of entertainment figures. Publishers are accustomed to books being sold to them as a package, with a ghost and author already teamed-up, ready to collaborate on a fully realised project, complete with marketing strategy too.

Today, ghosts are used to write anything and everything, from 140-word tweets, to speeches, to lengthy biographies. There are entire content mill marketplaces where writers vie to pen cheap copy to fill company websites. Well-known businessmen use ghost written books as a calling card to reinforce their expertise in a particular area (after all, if they have published a book they *must* know what they are talking about). Books are used as a marketing tool to expand on an expert's knowledge and crowd-pulling power.

Ghosting has even been immortalised in film, with the Roman Polanski's thriller, *The Ghost*, which was adapted by the Robert Harris book of the same name. In it former Prime Minister Adam Lang, played by Pierce Brosnan, enlists the ghost, played by Ewan McGregor, to write his memoirs. Ewan's character is somewhat significantly never given a name in the film, emphasising that ghosts don't really exist.

'So, how do we go about this?' asks Lang, early on in the film, clearly bemused by the whole process and not a little disinterested. The line comes not long after the abrupt greeting to his collaborator: 'Who are you?'

'I interview you and turn your answers into prose,' is the somewhat dry reply from the newly recruited ghost.

This exchange perhaps does the most to neatly summarise the art of a ghostwriter. They listen to a subject who can't, or doesn't want to, record their version of events and then turn it into an interesting and commercial product that everyone wants to read, all in exchange for a (hopefully) decent fee. Under this arrangement, the author's legacy will be established forever in print and most of the time the wider population is none the wiser about a hired hand's involvement. For all intents and purposes, a ghost doesn't exist.

But they do exist and today they are all around us.

CHAPTER ONE
WHY USE A GHOST?

The first question anyone considering a collaboration might be asking themselves is: do I really need a ghost at all? For many people, particularly those in the public eye, the answer is usually clear cut. They may even get approached by a publisher and asked the question:

'Mr (or Ms) celebrity, would you consider letting us publish your autobiography?'

Implicit in the offer is an understanding a package will be put together to make the process as smooth as humanly possible and that will naturally include the offer of a ghost to pen their story.

Alternatively, a well-known personality might be persuaded by advisors to write a book as part of a wider marketing push and will be told professional help is integral to its success. As publisher Trevor Dolby at Preface, puts it, they've done the calendar, they've put out the 'best of' DVD and embarked on the 16-date UK tour, so now it is time for the book.

It is the next logical step to promote the brand. Usually though, when agents suggest it, the personality

will say: 'yeah, great, as long as I don't have to write it'. In many ways these books are not books at all. They look like books, but they are a piece of merchandise. It is part of buying the t-shirt and the rest of it. It is all part of the career-end of things.

That doesn't mean it doesn't have to be good though. That old adage of churn it out, they won't care, isn't true here. The end-product has to be their voice, it has to reflect what the fans are seeing on the television, or reading in social media. It has to be as clever, assiduous and detailed as anything else. You can't take the mickey out of people. That is very important and why you need a ghost writer.

What then for mere mortals who don't have publishers offering tempting deals, or advisors pushing the idea? Why write a book and why use a ghost?

Let's tackle the reasons to write a book to begin with. There are a multitude of reasons for producing a book. The first one most people cite is to earn money. This is usually the point where ghosts will hopefully step in and dissuade a would-be author when they are approached on a collaboration. While bestselling books can be highly lucrative, there are thousands that never make a penny.

No, there needs to be more pressing reasons.

The author may be an expert in their field, for example, and want to tell the world about it. A book reinforces a person's credibility because it makes them a name in a given area and being the 'go to' expert increases their visibility and earning power.

There may, however, be more personal reasons, such as relating a story of a difficult period, a tragedy or an injustice. Some authors find relating their experiences an important part of the healing process.

Occasionally, authors will be unclear about what it is they want to write. They know there is a book inside them, or at least a burning desire to write one and leave a legacy in words, but they are just not sure what it is about. People like this may need their ideas teased out, sorted through and assessed for their interest value to a wider audience.

Once anyone makes up their mind they want to write a book and reflect that a ghost might just be what they need to make it happen, it is time to weigh up what a ghost will mean to the success, or otherwise, of a completed book. After all, a ghost won't be free and while we discuss the different payment options later in the book, it is important to think about the financial implications from the off.

If an author is relying on securing a publishing deal working with a ghost could make all the difference between success and failure. That is certainly the view of leading literary agent Andrew Lownie.

I often tell would-be authors, particularly those with real life stories, they probably won't get placed if they don't work with a ghost. Plus, if they do get picked up, a good collaboration should double their advance.

The other way of looking at it is, as well as securing a bigger advance, a ghost could actually save an author money. If the named author is a public figure, or even just a busy person, they will probably be doing ok and making money out of their day job. Devoting four hours a day to writing just won't be cost effective when they might make a considerable amount more for public speaking, or doing what they do. If they carry on doing what they are good at, while handing over the book writing to a ghost, it should work well for both sides.

Once they start thinking about giving up a large part of their advance, or paying a fee to a ghost, some authors do get cold feet and begin to wonder if they would be better off writing it themselves. After all, anyone at the top of their profession, as a TV celebrity, politician, or businessman, is likely to be pretty eloquent. Similarly, anyone of those ordinary folks with an extraordinary story would surely be best placed to tell it. So, why do so many people turn to ghosts?

The first, and most obvious reason, is time. As Jonathan Taylor, Headline Publishing group's publishing director says;

In an absolutely ideal world, all of our 'famous names' would have the time and craft to write their own books beautifully. But very often they have neither, so ghosts are completely necessary. Self-written celebrity memoirs are very rare animals.

Planning, structuring and writing a 80,000 word-plus book is no easy undertaking even for someone who does it for a living. Even working full time, it can take ghosts up to three months to finish a book. It can take more time than that if the subject is more complex and requires a lot of research. So, time is a real factor. Anyone who is busy with a job, running a business, helping with family or just living their life, might struggle with setting aside up to four hours a day to write their story. Or, as many aspiring writers find, they might start off with good intentions and then rapidly find real life intervenes.

Discipline is another major reason why many people don't give book writing a go themselves. They just can't ever seem to find the right time to sit down and get the words out. Even if they do vow to set aside an hour a day in the first flush of enthusiasm, it is never long before a distraction or two slips in and the book gets put on the back burner. Before they know it, they won't have touched their novel for weeks and the momentum will be lost. For a ghost, on the other hand, it is their full time job. If they don't write 1000 words a day, or 2000, or whatever target they set themselves, that ghost won't make a living. If they don't finish a manuscript, they won't be paid. That always concentrates the mind.

None of this is to say a ghosted book requires no time commitment whatsoever from the named author. It does. For a truly successful collaboration the author needs to meet their ghost on a regular basis either in person, or by phone, or via Skype. If a book is to make any progress, it has to be given the time it deserves. Working with a ghost will shorten the time investment for the named author, but it won't do away with it altogether.

Closely aligned to time and discipline is the element of skill required to pen a book. Some people assume anyone can write so it stands to reason they could get their story down if given enough time. If they are talking about the pure mechanics of getting a sufficient number of words written, they'd probably be right. But, knowing what to write and presenting it in an engaging, thoughtful and sustained way that will keep a reader hooked for chapter-after-chapter, that's a different proposition entirely. As one leading publisher admits; 'A lot of celebrities today don't have the vocabulary, imagination, or skill to make their jottings into something that is halfway readable. The same goes for would-be tellers of real life stories.' It's a brutal assessment but, knowing what to write and tailoring it to a reader's needs in a way that keeps their attention, isn't easy.

Another, perhaps less considered aspect of book writing, is whether or not the subject actually enjoys writing at all. Sure, there aren't many people on the planet who wouldn't like to airily hand you a paperback and say that's their latest novel, but would they actually see themselves sitting down for hours on end, agonising over writing, plot development or structure?

While most business leaders and politicians and a fair smattering of celebrities would quite rightly argue they have the verbal skills to produce a compelling piece of writing, there is a big leap between writing an interesting 'think piece' for a magazine, or a report for colleagues, or a first person review and producing an interesting, 80,000 word book. Writing a well-structured work of this length is a huge undertaking. It can take some ghosts years to perfect their style to the stage where they are regularly published. Even veterans will have experienced rejections and extensive edits in their past. It is difficult to write a book, which is why there are ghosts in the first place.

There are also more aspects to book writing than simply knowing how to construct a sentence. Often there is a large amount of careful and time-consuming background research that needs to be done too. This is certainly the case in anything other than a straight biography, or true-life tale where the author is simply relating their own story. This might happen when, say, a well-known figure is invited to write on a subject they are associated with, rather than on something they have seen or done first hand. In January 2014, for example, actress Gillian Andersen, best known for her role as FBI Agent Dana Scully, Agent Fox Mulder's sceptical partner in the hit sci-fi series The X Files, announced she was writing a series of sci-fi books with a collaborator. She said at the time her nine years of living in a 'semi-science-fictional universe' gave her an ingrained knowledge, but conceded her co-writer Jeff Rovin brought in the sci-fi expertise.[1] Andersen is undoubtedly a great actress,

1   X-Files star Gillian Andersen to write science fiction novels, The Guardian, 15 January 2014

but she was big enough to admit she needed help to produce a convincing book on 'her' subject.

For the sake of literary variety, it is a great thing that it's not just actors who want to cast their nets further afield and therefore turn to ghosts. While first time authors are often advised to write what they know about, perhaps drawing upon their knowledge or experiences in the field, this doesn't always follow. After all, it would be a pretty dull world if a civil servant from Croydon only wrote about being a civil servant in Croydon, or a horticulturist chose to concentrate on the trials and tribulations of tilling the land. We'd certainly never have had great novels such as *Hitchhikers Guide, Watership Down* or *The War of The Worlds*, which explore subjects beyond our everyday life. Thankfully many authors have more ambitious plans for their work and are happy to work with ghosts to display their versatility by tackling subjects out of their comfort zone. This can be challenging for a ghost, but with the right collaborator it can work out well for both sides. This was the experience of David Long who is both a ghost and an author in his own right. He collaborated with a well-known businessman who he only identifies as an 'internet squillionaire'. The book in question was not biographical, or even based on the author's successful career. Instead it focussed on environmental issues, a subject close to the author's heart.

He is very clever and imaginative entrepreneur, rather than a scientist and constantly came up with all sorts of wacky ideas about how the world could be

made a much better place. My job was to go away and validate his theories by doing my own research, or by speaking to an expert in the field. Then every fortnight or so, I would go back and argue the case with him. Often he would completely disagree with what I had uncovered, so I would have to go and find yet more evidence. That is how we bashed out the book.

Long's experience demonstrates another important characteristic which is essential for good collaboration between author and ghost: perspective. If the entrepreneur in the example above had the time it would have been very easy for him to jot down his own musings with very little scrutiny. The fact a well-known businessman was motivated enough to write his own blueprint for environmental nirvana may well have been enough to attract the interest, or at the very least curiosity, of a publisher. However, had David Long not argued over the substance of each point and repeatedly validated or refuted the arguments the author was putting forward, it is quite unlikely the book would ever have seen the light of day. Any publisher would have taken a look at the raw copy and dismissed it as unsubstantiated nonsense.

Working with a third party brings a fresh viewpoint to a story, which is something any author needs, however well they know their subject. Ghosts automatically have distance from an author. When someone shares their memories with a co writer it is the equivalent of stepping back, looking over everything and judging what is important from a reader's point of view. It's hard to do that when you've been fully immersed in something for years and years, particularly if it is an emotionally gruelling subject. A ghost can steer a story in the right direction. They will see what holes need filling in a narrative, what might be important to a reader and what isn't, where there are obvious flaws in characterisations or settings and what elements the author might need to consider beefing up. In short, they'll say what they think the book *really is* about as opposed to what the author *thinks* it is.

It is quite hard to get this rational perspective when you are close to a subject and that is why inexperienced authors can get bogged down in irrelevant detail of a story. An even worse tendency is for an author to get so carried away that they see their book as a tailor-made opportunity to settle a score or two, as Louise Dixon, a senior editorial director at Michael O'Mara books found:

We had one instance of a personality who was writing his own book and the end result was fabulous, but we couldn't publish it. It was all about his family and was terribly uncomplimentary and totally actionable. If we took out all the bits about the family we would have had no book left at all. Our lawyer told us if we published we would be sued.

Publishers are a lot more cautious today and we have to be. There have been so many high profile legal cases. Privacy is one issue you can be really hanged for but most lay people don't understand it. They'll say, but the event in question definitely happened

and it was all over the newspapers at the time. I have to tell them that doesn't mean it can be written in a book. In the eyes of the law a book is seen as a more formal document with longevity, whereas a newspaper will be the next day's chip wrapper. A ghost would know that, while a less experienced author probably won't.

This is where the professionalism a ghost brings in is so important. They know about privacy and confidentiality and all those other issues we have to skirt around in some way or another. They can come to the publisher early on and say something like; I am not sure how far we can go down this road talking about Aunty Val being a raging drunk.

Considering legal aspects of publishing might seem dull when writing a gripping opus of triumph over adversity, or of loves won and lost, but it can't be ignored. Again, a decent ghost will come into their own here and will be able to advise on such thorny subjects as copyright law, libel, defamation, warranties and, of course, privacy.

Are there any downsides to working with a ghost, aside from the cost? Some people might be reluctant to hire one because they are worried that handing over their story might damage their credibility. A public figure might be nervous that their potential readers would question why they can't do it themselves. They can probably almost hear them saying: aren't they up to the job? How hard can it be? The knowledge that ghosting is an anonymous pursuit won't assuage their fears, even though very often the reader has no idea that the person who wrote the book and the person with their name on the cover are not one and the same.

Generally though, the presence of a ghost is something only known to the author, their ghost and the publisher. More importantly, no one among the book-buying public really cares either way, says Weidenfeld & Nicolson publisher Alan Samson. Indeed, most readers expect high profile books to be ghosted these days and take it as a sign of good quality. The downside for publishers like Samson is readers are often sceptical when some celebrity authors insist it is all their own work.

Whenever I give a talk on publishing, which is about two or three times a year, there is always a large intake of breath from the audience about the notion that celebrities can write their own book. One quality broadsheet newspaper did a rather mean piece, naming three of my authors as those who used ghosts when they had actually written their own work. I tried to tell them not every celebrity book is ghosted, but it fell on deaf ears.

If a celebrity wants to write their own books I would always encourage them. Rather like lawyers, actors know the weight and value of words. That is why many write their own books and love doing so. Sometimes with time constraints it is not always possible and that is when ghosts can be very useful.

Authors who are worried about ceding too much control in the writing of their story can explore other options that take advantage of the skills a ghost can offer, yet also allow an element of artistic input from the person with their name on the dust jacket. Ghost writing has changed a lot in recent years. Traditionally, the role of a ghost was to sit with the author, listen to their story and then go away and write it into a coherent book. The lines are more blurred now. Some authors opt to write at least part of their books themselves and may only bring in a professional to help shape or structure their work. Others may even write an entire manuscript, only turning to a ghost at the end for a 'hard edit' to get it into a more user-friendly form. These 'ghostwriter lite' options allow authors to benefit from the fresh perspective of another writer, but also afford a sense of closer involvement.

HarperCollins non fiction publisher Natalie Jerome says this approach is in line with the evolution of the rest of the publishing industry in recent years. Ghosting has become much more of a collaborative process where authors are more likely to pick and choose the skills they need.

People increasingly want to be more involved in the writing, even if they don't have the time or the skill to produce a whole book. This is certainly the case with more high profile authors. The worlds of the editor and ghost are blurring; our roles are more fluid now.

Some ghosts, such as Andrew Croft, for example, encourage authors to get some of their own story down in the early stages. He sees it as a way to help concentrate their thought process.

I always urge people to give it a go first, just to see if they can do it. It is a way of getting them to get the story down in a coherent way. Whatever they come up with will be very useful material for the ghost when the time comes and they'll know what questions to ask when the tape recorder is switched on.

It may work out very well for them and it may even turn out that they may only need to hire an editor at the end. There is, after all, a very fine line between ghosting and editing.

This is by no means a universal view among ghosts though. Other ghosts say it is distracting trying to incorporate each and every element introduced in an author's notes. It is much easier to begin afresh. This difference in style demonstrates there is a case for choosing a collaborator carefully. Every author is different and so is every ghost. Any author would be advised to put as much effort into choosing their co-writer as in weighing up the pros and cons for using one at all.

Ghostwriters are not for every aspiring author but for many, deciding to use a ghost is a shrewd choice, particularly if they've tried writing a book themselves but never got anywhere. It allows the author to concentrate on other priorities while a professional writer does what is needed to bring a story alive.

Chapter Two
Why publishers like ghosts

The Oxford dictionary defines an 'author' as the writer of a book, article, or document. It also says an author can be the *originator* of a plan or idea. While the majority of readers assume the first interpretation, the book trade is quite happy to accept the second. This is why it is seen as perfectly acceptable that the vast majority of books authored by a celebrity or politician are written with the help of a ghost. It is also why the practice is common in a growing number of other publishing genres, from business books to real life stories. The named author comes up with the direction of the project and the credibility to promote it, while the co writer does the writing.

Although it is impossible to know the true scale of ghosting, because many writers sign non-disclosure agreements, industry estimates are that up to 50 per cent of non-fiction bestseller lists are ghosted and when a major celebrity or politician is involved, that figure can rise to near 100 per cent. After all, if an executive or performer can earn millions a year doing the day job, they will hardly want to put it all on hold for three months or more to write a book. They let a ghost take care of that.

It is these big names that publishers want in the main part too. Winning the rights to publish an 'A' lister's memoir is the nearest the book trade gets to a sure fire thing. Get it right and the books will fly off the shelf just on the strength that they are the latest musings from whatever figure is currently in the public eye. And publishers need these hits, because they feed the system. Each bestseller by David Beckham, or Alex Ferguson pays for the other books on the list that make a loss. It is worth noting, publishers don't always get it right in this numbers game. Sales of Pippa Middleton's book *Celebrate* were reported to be dire, shifting just 18,000 copies when it first launched. Pippa was thought to be hot property after the Royal wedding between her sister Kate and Prince William in 2011 and was paid a reported £400,000 advance by Penguin. The book on entertaining was dubbed 'terrible' by bestselling writer Jilly Cooper[2] and derided for being banal by critics. It might be churlish to point out, but she didn't use a ghost either, apparently.

Although selling a celebrity book is (usually) straight forward, publishers do want to discover new talent. For the business model to work, they need a steady stream of new authors coming through and there is always the hope any new discovery will develop into the next JK Rowling. Of course, finding the next

---

2 Pippa Middletons book is terrible, says Jilly Cooper, The Telegraph, 2 December 2012.

big thing isn't easy, especially in non-fiction. Selling a book by a new name, even if it is bang on the money in terms of the zeitgeist, is a risk. Consumers don't know they'll like a book until they try it, so it is often safer to return to the same author again and again. If you've got any doubts about that being true, you only have to look at the experience of JK Rowling, whose mystery novel *Cuckoo's Calling*, under the pseudonym Robert Galbraith, only sold 1,500 copies. Once it was leaked it was the work of the woman behind *Harry Potter* the book became an overnight bestseller.

The reliance on big-selling celebrity novels has in recent years spawned another interesting trend; celebrity ghosts. Publishing observers say it all kicked off in the early Eighties when William Novak, a then struggling writer, received a modest advance to pen *Iacocca*, an autobiography of American businessman Lido Anthony 'Lee' Iacocca famed for his revival of the struggling Chrysler Corporation. The book became a monster bestseller, becoming one of the all-time leaders in hardcover nonfiction sales. While Novak never got a penny in royalties for the millions of copies sold, his success sparked a boom in ghost-written celebrity memoirs. From that moment on, Novak was the first point of call for many publishers looking to pair a celebrity with a ghost and he has worked with Nancy Reagan, Oliver North, and Magic Johnson at a spiralling rate of fees. The fact that Novak's name is always paired on the cover with the main author is not the only sign of how acceptable

ghosting has become. Publishers use the involvement of 'star' ghosts like Novak, to boast of a book's
credentials. When Bill Clinton's former aide George
Stephanopoulos persuaded Novak to pen his memoir in the late 1990s, the New York Times announced
that having a well-known ghost had become 'a mark
of prestige like being seen about town with a trophy
wife.' Times Journalist and author Chris Ayres, who
ghosted Ozzy Osbourne's 2009 memoir '*I am Ozzy*',
said in one interview that who you choose as your collaborator is seen as almost part of the talent of the
artist. He said; 'It's seen as a decision that's an important part of the creative process.'[3]

New York literary agent Madeleine Morel, who
represents more than 100 ghostwriters, says the
major consideration is producing commercially viable books.

**So many books aren't books any more, they are
products. I've had countless conversations with artist's managers who say: we need a book by so and so. I
say: great, what is the book? They say: we don't know,
we are going to explore it and figure it out on the way.**

**The book is a product they have to have. A lot of
this is dictated by the fact we have all become slaves
to pop culture. It is very unromantic.**

It might sound unromantic, but putting interesting high profile people together with decent writers
to produce a commercial product does make a lot of

---

3   Famous get published with a little help from these ghosts,
Chicago Sun-Times, 14 February 2010.

business sense. Books are a product and are already a team effort, where editors, publishers, agents and designers get involved. A ghost is just part of the package.

In 1994, for example, Chris Owen, who was Naomi Campbell's agent at the Elite model agency, approached publisher William Heinemann. Campbell had already produced an album, *babywoman* and Owen, himself a former publishing sales rep, could see the value of producing a book under the super-model's name. Campbell said at the time she 'did not have the time to sit down and write a book' so Caroline Upcher, then an editor at Heinemann and a novelist in her own right, was contracted to write *Swan,* a glitzy book about the fashion industry. There was virtually no collaboration between Campbell and Upcher; the idea was simply to use the name. It is the book publishing equivalent of a celebrity promoting a fashion line, or perfume, which in reality they had little or no hand in creating. As Caroline recalls, it was a fairly surreal experience.

I took it on rather like a piece of journalism, but I had a ball at the same time. I insisted on doing an enormous amount of research, which of course meant fully immersing myself in the fashion busi-ness. Naomi didn't want much to do with the whole project but she was incredibly helpful in opening all sorts of doors for me. I got into fashion shows in London, Paris and New York and spent six months sitting in the office of the Elite modelling agency in

London. When Eileen Ford, the founder of the Ford model agency in New York heard what I was doing, she invited me in straight away.

It wasn't ghosting in the purest sense at all. In fact, I hardly saw Naomi and she had minimal input. The only time she got upset was the one time I did inadvertently write something that came perilously close to her own life story. She said she didn't want it to be about her at all.

It got quite funny at one point. Naomi was having talks with Harvey Weinstein's American film company Miramax, so she asked me to meet with her at the Halkin in Belgravia to give her an update on the plot of the book and the various characters. When I got to her room, we spent some time admiring her new navel ring and then there wasn't much time to go over the book. I joined her downstairs in the lobby while she met with two women from Miramax. I just sat there, ready to jump in with backup details of the book if she floundered, but she never did. I wasn't actually introduced and I have often wondered who on earth they thought I was.

If a person appeals to book buyers on the strength of their fame, wealth, or power that is a great starting point, but ghosts are invaluable in providing writing skills if they are incapable of getting their story on the page. Indeed, according to one leading non-fiction publisher Trevor Dolby at Preface, ghosts come into their own when it comes to working with big names because occasionally celebrities are completely dysfunctional.

Look at it this way. You have a supreme talent, who has got to where they have because they are the best at what they do in the country, or even the world. If anyone reaches this stage, even if it is only a brief period, it can completely skew their view of the rest of the world and the way it works around them. It is not easy to work with someone like that, let alone get a good book out of them.

Equally, when someone is a supreme actor or sportsman, their whole personality is sometimes subsumed into their particular talent. It is not like the bell curve of a normal person who might be reasonably good at most things, probably relatively balanced with a bit of common sense. Every part of their personality can be crushed into this amazing talent they have. Either side of it though, they may be completely dysfunctional.

As a publisher, you have to cater for that and a ghost solves a lot of problems. Obviously a key skill of any ghost is an infinite supply of patience. They have to be an author's friend and confidant and make them feel OK about revealing their lives and idiosyncrasies to them. That is the skill we need.

Ghosts do indeed take out some of the hassle of dealing with some more challenging authors. It is a ghost writer's lot to be an interviewer, therapist and friend to their subjects because, often quite understandably, delving into the intricate detail of a person's life is not always easy for either party, particularly if there are some dark secrets to discuss. The author has already lived through it once and may be reluctant to do so again. Tensions can boil over, tempers can flair and tears can and do flow. It is up to a ghost to keep it all on track, managing the delicate balancing act of teasing out the necessary detail without distressing their subject unduly. The experience can take its toll and not surprisingly some publishers and indeed agents would prefer to keep this side of the process at arms length.

To take an extreme example, one ghost, let's call him James, penned a book in the name of a woman who had multiple personality disorder. She was a fascinating subject who had an emotional and heartwarming story to tell of her own personal triumph over extreme adversity. However, as anyone would imagine, she was quite high maintenance as a subject. Indeed, she was on the phone to James morning, noon and night, sometimes shouting, sometimes wailing with grief, sometimes happily chatting away and every time utterly oblivious to the impact it was having on James.

Another ghost, Mark, told how a subject would regularly call him at all hours and rant: 'You are being paid to get inside my head, well this is what it is like in there!'

It doesn't happen in every book project, but at least occasionally, ghostwriters have to be prepared to be their subject's punch bags, which is something no publisher is prepared to do.

Publishers are agreed that a major catalyst for the increased use of ghosts today is widespread demand for higher standards of literary work. The trend that has most influenced this shift is the popularity of so-called misery memoirs which came out of nowhere in the mid Nineties and began selling in phenomenal numbers. Most observers credit the American writer Dave Pelzer for beginning this trend when he published his story of his outrageously cruel childhood in his memoir *A Child Called It.* In the book, he details how his alcoholic mother, who dismissed him as 'an it', beat, starved, stabbed and burned him, forced him to swallow ammonia and eat the contents of his siblings' nappies. It rapidly became a runaway bestseller, selling millions of copies, spawning two sequels and a number of related books.

Misery lit, which is somewhat coyly referred to as 'Painful Lives' in Waterstones, 'Tragic Lives' in WH Smith and 'Real Lives' in Borders, very quickly became what has been described as 'the book world's biggest boom sector'[4]. As much as 30 per cent of the non-fiction charts in every given week is made up from grinding misery. The genre has created a whole new market for ghosts who have the skill to interpret these stories. Interestingly though, according to Weidenfeld & Nicolson publisher Alan Samson, it upped the ante across the whole publishing sector. Readers tend no longer to be satisfied with the glossy,

---

4 Mis Lit: Misery is book world's biggest boom sector, Independent, Anthony Barnes, March 4 2007.

marketing-led, PR-sanctified versions of famous people's lives. Fame alone won't sell a story. They want to know the whole, unvarnished, gritty truth about the celebrities they adore.

When I was a young editor, many celebrities used their books as a form of career management. So in their book they had never had to overcome any obstacles, everything in their life had gone swimmingly well, and everybody was lovely. It was the equivalent of: I sang with Sammy Davis Junior, or Frank Sinatra, and it was all so wonderful. The sales of these books reflected the fact they were career management and not terribly interesting. This meant that ghosts were often poorly paid and the standard wasn't brilliant.

A Boy Called It by Dave Peltzer was a turning-point book. It didn't merely introduce the whole concept of misery memoirs; it began a trend that filtered into celebrity publishing. Readers no longer wanted the fluff. Autobiography has become more about the obstacles the author has overcome, whether it is a family upset, or some trauma like a terrible accident, or even in some cases a bad haircut. Readers demanded that celebrities become much more open. Ghosting had to change and there was a need for writers who were more skilled at teasing the detail out and who could present it in a compelling way.

The rise of misery lit is not the only phenomenon that has led to a demand for more skilled writers. The rise and rise of social media has been another significant influence. Today, modern celebrities blog, tweet, message and post endless minutiae about their daily lives on-line. It is not just part of the PR package, it is a vital component. After all, why wait for a publicist to organise a press briefing to refute a rumour when it is possible to do the job yourself with a few clicks of a cell phone. (As an aside, ghost Twittering has become an art form of its own, but this breed of cyber ghosts are very invisible indeed. Celebrities are not keen to own up to subcontracting this particular aspect of their innermost 'thoughts'.)

With no detail of some public figure's lives sacred, however intimate, there is a huge appetite for these communications among fans. The natural knock-on effect is a change in the way ordinary people feel about celebrities they follow. Thanks to the daily drip feed of information they believe they know their idols just as well as any one of their real life acquaintances. If a celebrity who has been this active in the blogosphere then released a book of half-baked anecdotes, or worse still, ones that have already been well rehearsed online, it is not going to cut it with readers. No, they demand authentic, well crafted, interesting and absolutely fresh revelations.

Publisher Trevor Dolby at Preface says it all comes down to trust and woe betide any publisher who misjudges the passion of fans when it comes to 'their' celebrities.

There was a time when celebrities and their handlers thought: we'll just turn the handle and it will be fine. They were happy to repeat the same old stuff.

Fans won't buy into that today. They believe, rightly or wrongly, they know and understand people they follow and have to hear their true voice come through in everything they read. A book won't get anywhere unless the fans feel they can trust and understand the writer.

Any book from a well-known name, therefore, has to offer something much, much, more to capture the imagination of the book-buying public and this is where an experienced ghost is worth their weight in gold. By the same token though, it is more imperative than ever that the voice in a ghosted book sounds like the voice the fans know and love.

Of course, ghost Tweeters notwithstanding, the other side of the coin is those in the public eye do feel more in control of their message today. If they haven't handed their online personality over to someone else, it is probably because they enjoy the close connection they have with their followers. They are confident about being themselves, and likely to work in a far more collaborative way with their co writers. The skill of a ghost in this case is to expand their message, find fresh and interesting things to say, and maintain the interest of the main author.

The book industry relies on the fact a ghost won't just write down what the named author tells them but they will push hard to get something new. It takes a skilled questioner to cut through the easy laughs or glossy PR persona, rummage through a person's innermost thoughts and judge what is really worth

listening to. Similarly, it takes an experienced interviewer to gently steer a subject away from using their
book as a platform for point scoring, exaggerated
versions of key episodes or unwarranted (probably
misguided) self analysis. An experienced ghost will
keep a story fresh because they are prepared to ask
the really intimate questions.

Not all authors accept the need for a ghost at all.
While some are indeed capable of writing their stories
themselves, most could benefit from working alongside a specialist writer. Deborah Crewe, an ex-civil
servant turned ghost-writer, who worked with politician Jack Straw on his biography *Last Man Standing:
Memoirs of a Political Survivor*[5] said it took 18-months
of 'badgering' to persuade him to share the load.

**I knew Jack's wife from my work as a civil servant
and when I saw Jack was thinking about writing a book
I got in touch straight away. It took a lot of patient
badgering from all sides before he would accept
there might be a useful role I could play. Once he
did agree that I could be involved though, it quickly
became clear we were going to work well together.**

**Part of the issue had been that Jack knew he didn't
want a ghostwriter: he wanted to write the book himself, which indeed he did. So my role with this book
was not a ghosting one at all. I did a huge amount of
research, especially on Jack's time as Home Secretary
(I had worked in the Home Office myself). Jack wrote**

---

5   Last Man Standing: Memoirs of a Political Survivor, by Jack
Straw, Macmillan, September 2012

the first drafts. I then knocked them into shape, co-ordinating comments, doing first edits, and working with Jack's Commons' Researcher.

Sometimes this meant line editing and at other times it was more structural. For example, early on, there was a section that Jack seemed particularly wedded to, but I found slowed the pace of the book. It was a long narrative about a David and Goliath battle between commoners and landowners over the future of Epping Forest (where Jack was raised). It was genuinely very interesting, but it did go on a bit and it wasn't really his story. I told him that. So did the editor at Pan Macmillan. He was a bit taken aback because he really loved it, but after a lively discussion we took it out. After that, when he went on at length about anything, I'd say 'I think this is a bit "Epping Forest"'.

I also kept Jack to his extremely tight writing deadlines, earning myself the lovely title of Ms SD (Slave Driver).

While many writers come to understand and accept a ghost's involvement over time, some do not and many ghosts can relate experiences of clashes with frustrated would be authors.

As one ghost, let's call her Sally, describes: 'Everything was going swimmingly when we first met and did the interviews, but I did detect a certain resentment. When I started sending draft chapters over, she really kicked off. She sent back page after page, with line-by-line corrections, demanding

I sent back revisions by return. It was obvious there was a deep-seated resentment about using a ghost at all. It was never going to work out and I had to tell the publisher that too. I'm not sure if another ghost was brought in, but I haven't seen her book on the shelves yet.'

If publishers believe ghosting is an acceptable sign of quality among celebrity authors, what of less well-known writers? Does a pairing with a ghost help or hinder a project? While it is now accepted that a key benefit of ghostwriting is it helps stories be told that otherwise might never come out, the other side of this is that to get that story out to the widest possible audience, the first step is to attract a publisher.

Publishers see thousands of manuscripts cross their desks every week, many claiming to be *the* definitive work on this subject or that. The trouble is, with so many definitive works jostling for attention in near identical subject areas, it isn't easy to stand out as an author. The odds are further stacked against success if the writer is not particularly well known, has no evidence of a track record with previous definitive works, or indeed any substantial written work whatsoever. A collaboration with a ghost writer could therefore smooth a book's passage through from the proposal stage to finished manuscript. Indeed, as we saw in the previous chapter, industry experts say it increases the chances of a publishing deal considerably.

Take a work of non-fiction, for example. If the author is not an out-and-out A list celebrity that any publisher would give their right arm to sign, they will have quite a lot to prove. They won't get close to securing a meeting with a publisher, let alone a coveted publishing deal, unless they can demonstrate two things. The first is that they are an expert in their field, because that will play well in marketing and promotion and ensure book sales. If a publisher can't see any evidence of a prospective market there is very little chance they'll invest. The book trade needs to be convinced putative buyers respect and will probably therefore seek out the author. Then, secondly, the would-be author has to reassure a publisher the book in question will be well written and structured in a way that will grip the attention of book buyers and reviewers. Even better, is a book that is written so well it is highly likely to be recommended to all the book buyers' friends. A well-known ghost, or at least one with a good track record, will answer this second criteria. Having a professional on board signals a seriousness about a project.

Even if ghosts are broadly acceptable, and indeed welcomed, by publishers, there is always a delicate balancing act between acknowledging the presence of a ghost and maintaining the illusion it is all the work of the author. Sidgwick & Jackson editorial director Ingrid Connell, for example, prefers not to credit ghosts on the cover.

It can undermine the credibility of a book. A ghost could talk themselves out of a job if they insist on credit like that, definitely. I do sometimes offer to put

the ghost on the title page – it depends on the book and how the author feels about giving the ghost this credit. However, it is right the author does acknowledgements and thanks the ghost in words that make it clear that the ghost wrote it. The ghost needs to be able to show people that this is their work. That is fair enough. But to have it on the cover? It looks wrong.

Most publishers favour the word 'collaboration', which slightly fudges the issue and gives the impression, at least to the outside world, of an entirely equal division of labour. As long as neither party out-and-out deny this is the case, this usually seems to suffice. It doesn't insult the intelligence of the reader, the image of the author is preserved and the ghost is rewarded for a job well done. There is no deception involved and no one really minds.

From a publisher's point of view, the very best ghosting collaborations are the ones where ghost and author work together like a well oiled machine and the process is so smooth the named author actually begins to believe the work is 100 per cent theirs. It is an experience Preface's Trevor Dolby welcomes.

If an author is happy to go on TV shows and describe in great detail how they sat down each morning with a blank sheet of paper and what a trial it all was writing their account of their story, I am happy. That means the ghost has done a great job. The author believes in the book so much and has been so immersed in the process, they genuinely believe they did it. That is a great collaboration.

CHAPTER THREE
WHO PAYS AND HOW MUCH?

Stories abound of multi million pound or dollar book advances paid to celebrities. In 2006, football star Wayne Rooney then aged just 21, signed the largest sporting book deal in history when he agreed to write five books in 12 years for HarperCollins for a £5 million advance. Publisher Little Brown and Company reportedly offered an eye-watering $7.3 million advance to Rolling Stones guitarist Keith Richards on the strength of a taster extract of his *Life* biography that was just ten pages long. Meanwhile, 'unknown' Celebrity Big Brother winner Chantelle Houghton bagged a £300,000 deal from Random House to write her biography just five months after winning the Channel Five reality show. Her fame at the time was based on the fact she wasn't, well, famous. She was planted into the TV series to fool fellow contestants into thinking she was in a make-believe band called Kandy Floss, when her only previous claim to fame was occasional work as a promotions girl.

Each of these names worked with a ghost writer to write the stories that earned the massive advances. Rooney snapped-up author and Beatles biographer Hunter Davies for his first book, *My Story So Far*, while Keith Richards worked with journalist James Fox on *Life* and Houghton warmly thanks Jean Richie for her writing skills in her acknowledgements for *Living The Dream, My Story*. With such huge figures on the table for celebrity books, it raises the very obvious question: do ghosts get a decent slice of this occasionally very big business?

The answer is a somewhat unsatisfactory; yes and no. The rewards for ghosting vary enormously. Some sought-after 'A' list ghosts with a track record of best-sellers behind them command as much as a million pounds or dollars per book, plus a share of royalties and a writing credit. The lowest tier of writer, sourced from freelancing websites such as Elance, will write a book for as little as £5000, or even less in some cases. In between these two levels are hundreds of ghosts with a bit of experience under their belts who expect between £15,000 and £50,000 or sometimes even more. It's difficult to get a more precise price list because ghostwriters usually sign non-disclosure agreements promising they will never reveal their involvement with a book, let alone what they got paid. However, on anecdotal evidence alone, surely this must be the most diverse pricing model in the business world?

There is, of course, a big element of 'buyer beware' here. In ghost writing, you really do get what you pay for. Experience and quality are, or at least should be, everything in book writing. It is virtually impossible to cut corners, do it on the cheap and still expect a readable book.

Look at it this way. We live in a world where shopping around is second nature. If anyone is buying, say, a set of golf clubs, they could find the keenest deal at the click of a mouse. So why not do the same to source a ghost? Click, click, click, hey, I've found one who will write my novel for less than £5000. Fantastic. Or is it?

When buying off-the-shelf goods like golf clubs, there are plenty of nifty little tricks to make them seem to be better value than they really are. Perhaps a bit of 'gold' plating here, a monogrammed logo there, a flashy, leather-coated bag and bingo, this collection of clubs looks just like a leading brand, yet set the buyer back a fraction of the usual cost. Who is to know? The problem is, you can't do the same with the written word. A skilled and experienced ghost knows how to structure a plot, build characters and grip the reader from the very first page. An unskilled, inexperienced ghost, won't. No amount of fancy chrome polish can disguise that fact. You can't pretend to produce a fantastic book.

Which brings us back to the how much does a ghost get paid question, although perhaps we should now insert 'decent', as in how much does a decent ghost get. In recent years, a large number of different ways to cut a deal with a collaborator have emerged. To explain the various ways a ghost gets paid, it may help to begin by going back to basics to first break down how the named author gets his or her money. After all, in most cases, the scale of the payment to a ghost is very much dependent upon and related to the advance the author receives, or the amount of money the author expects to make from their book.

Under the traditional publishing model, if a publisher is interested in buying a manuscript, it usually offers an advance against future royalty earnings. There is a little bit of alchemy involved here, but essentially what happens is a large number of people in the publishing house get together and work on all sorts of complex calculations to estimate how many copies they think they'll sell over a given period of time. An offer is usually made on this basis, although for the very biggest celebrities, a certain amount of incentive might occasionally be added to the price because otherwise they may not sign on the dotted line or could go elsewhere. After that, for every pound the author is paid, they have to earn that pound back in book sales *before* they can receive any additional royalty payments. So, in a highly simplistic interpretation, if an author were to get a £100,000 advance, with a royalty rate that worked out at £1 per book, they would have to sell 100,000 copies of their biography to pay off the advance. Once the publisher recoups the advance, they will pay royalties based on subsequent sales. These advances are guaranteed, so even if the book doesn't meet the publisher forecasts, the author keeps the cash.

With celebrity authors, particularly the big name ones, there is always a fair bit of discussion over how a ghost is remunerated once a publishing deal has been struck. It is common for ghosts to have their own agents today, so the celebrity's agent and the ghost writer's agent will have a tussle over whether the ghost will get a flat fee, or a percentage of the advance. Celebrity agents fight hard for flat fees, while most ghost writers' agents seek out a fifty fifty deal when they put their ghosts together with named authors. Of course, well-known, or previously successful, ghosts who are in demand are in a good position to negotiate. However, with some celebrities getting six figure advances or more, a straight fifty fifty split isn't always feasible. As one agent, Andrew Lownie explains, flexibility is always required.

A lot depends on the size of the advance. When there is a £200,000 plus deal, demanding half for a ghost may not be fair, particularly when the book is sold on the strength of the celebrity name, not just their story. In that case, it might be more appropriate for the ghost to get 25 per cent of the advance, or to negotiate royalties on a tapered level. Maybe the author gets a certain amount, the ghost gets another amount and after that the deal tapers in the interests of the subject.

Ghosts might like to note that, even if they do secure a fifty fifty deal, they will have to do some careful financial housekeeping. Publishing fees are usually split up into at least three tranches, so there will be a payment on signing, a payment when the manuscript is submitted and a payment when the book is published. As ghost Emma Murray notes, it can play havoc with finances.

I work for publishers in the US ; at first as a ghost but then as a co-author of academic textbooks for undergraduate and masters business courses. One particular publisher pays my advance in small instalments as I meet certain milestones. As a typical textbook can take up to two years from commissioning to publication, it can take that long to be paid fully which puts me under financial pressure. There are often delays on the publishing side which means months can go by without payment. To bridge this gap, I have to take on work on the side. It is impossible to live on what some publishers pay you up front, for more than a couple of months.

Traditional advances are by no means the only way ghost writing deals get cut today. In recent years, for example, some publishers will offer deals with no advance at all when there is less certainty about a project and how it will sell thanks to shifts in tastes in the market. Instead, they might offer an author and their ghost a joint share of 50 per cent of the receipts. This basically means that for each book that gets sold, the publisher gets half the receipt and the writing team get the other half. It is a way of encouraging the writers to share the risk and reward equally and can be a potentially lucrative option for ghosts.

A 'share of the risk' arrangement is very unusual in celebrity books, but is increasingly used in real life stories in various forms. Say a previously unknown author is looking for a professional writer to work with them on spec to pen a 'real life' memoir. In return for an equal share of any profit, a ghost will work with an author long before the treatment is shown to a publisher. It is a huge leap of faith on the ghost's behalf, because it means the professional writer will initially work for nothing on the understanding of a decent income down the line when the book sells. Before a publisher even considers the idea, a ghost will have to produce a full chapter-by-chapter break-down of what the book will cover, with a compelling summary, market information, details of other books in the genre and up to three complete chapters. Researching a proposal on this scale and drafting the requisite chapters is no small undertaking. Depending upon the complexity of the subject, it can take many hours of interviews with the author and a similar amount of time again to write it into a coherent and persuasive document. During this time, a ghost will not receive a penny of income and don't forget he or she has no certainty that the book will ever generate any money at all.

Very often the first proposal may not be the last either. As ghost Douglas Wight found when he began working with ex-soldier and police officer Ross Slater on his book *True Lies.*

Ross' story was very episodic. He'd been in the army, worked for the police and finally ended up in security, where he infiltrated Greenpeace as a double agent working for Special Branch. His career and life development and the various interesting things he had done seemed to fit in with the style of books that were popular when I was books editor at News of the World. However, by the time I came out of the newspaper and started to develop this idea, the trend had moved on to a very narrow focus on specific instances. No one picked up on the initial proposal based on his whole life. I had to start again and to narrow it down to the period at Greenpeace. That got publishers interested.

The expectation is that a ghost's expertise will help get the book noticed and, of course, in the best-case scenario the book will become a surprise bestseller guaranteeing a fantastic payday for all concerned. However, the other side of this argument is it may take many years for a book to take off, if at all. All the work may turn out to be for nothing.

For this on spec pricing model to work, a ghost has to choose the projects they do very carefully, be fully committed to a story and be prepared to be very patient. *The Girl with No Name: the Incredible True Story of a Child Raised by Monkeys,* by Marina Chapman, for example, a collaboration with ghost Lynne Barrett-Lee, took five years, with a number of twists and turns along the way, before it achieved its international bestselling status. Had Barrett-Lee not got involved though, the book might never have seen the light of day.

One of the biggest selling books I have been involved in is *Girl with No Name* but it took a long time to get anywhere. When I first came to the project, I thought I was the third ghost to work on it, but later found I was actually the sixth one for various reasons. The first three ghosts apparently didn't gel with the author, so it never got to the stage of a proposal going out. Then, two further ghosts got involved and wrote full proposals, neither of which sold.

I was asked to take a look at it and thought it was an amazing story. Even though I liked one of the earlier proposals, I changed it quite radically into a format I thought would sell.

It sold to a publisher in Australia first and then started picking up traction. After then attracting a modest offer from Mainstream in the UK, it went on to sell in a further eighteen countries and has been a hardback and paperback bestseller all around the world It was a real learning curve for me, but it showed that with the right treatment a story can prove its worth.

It takes a bit of faith from a ghost writer, but if you believe strongly enough in a story, then it is worth putting the time in because if you think it is good, it will hopefully pay eventually.

If I ever feel doubtful, I remind myself that publishers are not infallible. They sometimes get it wrong. There are only a very tiny number of them in quite a small clique, mainly in London. If they don't get fired up about a book, it doesn't happen, but as I have found out, that doesn't mean it isn't a good book that will sell well.

The problem for ghosts and would-be authors is there is no fixed price on a book. In a scenario where a ghost agrees to do a lot of work on spec for a equal share of any advance there is no way of knowing what a publisher might offer. Even a best guess is sometimes way off. Indeed, one publisher may decide a book is worth a paltry £4000 advance while another will make an offer of £40,000 for the same manuscript.

It is little wonder that ghosts are very choosy about the books they do on spec. They will invariably turn down many more projects than they agree to do. If a story doesn't look like it has a hope of commercial success it is unlikely to get ghosts rushing to support it.

Of course, it isn't always easy to tell if a book will attract interest from publishers. Indeed, as Douglas Wight found, having a celebrity name on the cover is no guarantee of success today. Douglas collaborated with film star Emily Lloyd on her autobiography *Wish I Was There*, a book he was convinced would have publishers queuing at the door.

Emily is clearly a well known name who has starred with 'A' listers such as Bruce Willis and Brad

Pitt. She was no flash in the pan. The feedback we kept getting from publishers though was she 'wasn't current'. One even suggested it might help if we got her on 'I'm a Celebrity' or another one of these reality shows. It was quite frustrating. We kept at it though and it worked out well because three publishers showed an interest in the end and it was a very rewarding exercise.

Sometimes though, ghosts may just take a punt if they truly believe a book will work. However, even if an author does have a book idea that interests a ghost enough to work on a collaborative basis, both parties will have to be prepared to be fairly creative to reduce the financial burden at this early, unpaid stage.

Katharine Quarmby says working closely with an author and 'cutting our cloth carefully' is often the choice between a book project getting off the ground, or being shelved altogether. The ghost, author and former BBC producer recently collaborated on a book about attempted forced marriage and honour crime that spanned Manchester to the Yemen. Although, in an ideal world, Quarmby would have immersed herself in the author's life and possibly even travelled with her to Yemen it just wasn't possible for a number of reasons.

As a ghost writer I have to decide what I can invest in a project up-front without any funding. I imagine that is going to be more and more the case for writers in the future. A lot of the good stories are going to come from places further afield and many may come from countries where it is not easy to visit for either political or financial reasons.

I had to travel up and down to Manchester quite a bit for this project, but we also did a lot by email and phone. We couldn't go out to Yemen together because it is far too dangerous [for the interviewee, as she was nearly murdered there], so we looked at home videos together and spent a long time discussing what it is like there. I asked my interviewee to try and imagine what it is like to be a tourist in that country. What is it like to go there for the first time and see everything? The reader is a tourist in a land they may never actually visit. We were not only just telling an adventure story, we are also enabling the reader to go to a country that few people will ever get the opportunity to experience. In a case like this I literally use Google maps and anything else I can lay my hands on to add value.

Luckily I also have contacts who have been to Yemen and even one good friend who has written a book about Yemen, so I asked them a lot of questions too. That all helped me get some political insight and some good wide context about what had happened to this woman without going to Yemen myself.

You have to do what you can.

Another way of structuring a deal with a ghost is for an author to pay them a flat fee, regardless of whether the finished book is picked up by a publisher. Here, the author will agree a fixed price up front with their ghost, which may or may not include a percentage share of any future royalties. Once again, there are many variables. The author may, for example, pay a ghost a fee of a few thousand pounds to write a book proposal and a few sample chapters to run by some publishers. Employing an experienced ghost might give an author a better chance of getting a publishing deal and a fair indication of its commercial potential. If the book is given a contract on the strength of the proposal, they can then renegotiate terms with the ghost, based on the advance they receive.

Alternatively, they may simply agree a flat fee up-front for the ghost to complete the whole book. The ghost will base their fee on the amount of time it will take them to write the manuscript and how much research and interviewing will be needed. Prices can vary wildly according to the experience of the ghost and can be anything from £10,000 to more than £100,000 depending on the complexity of the project.

A fee-based scenario like this is often most effective where an author already has a ready-made market for their books, is not reliant on a publishing advance and quite happy to self publish. They might be putting a book together as part of their own marketing package and will source a ghost in the same way as they would look for a graphic designer to lay out their book's pages, an editor to refine the copy and a printer to cover the production. Say the author was a business leader in a particular field and wanted to produce a book to demonstrate their expertise in a particular niche, such as sales or Human Resources. Being already well plugged into their target market, they'll be able to write, print, publish and market their work direct without the need of a publisher. They'll be in the perfect place to market their writing to potential customers via bespoke conferences, speaking engagements and trade PR. By taking control of the whole project, from ghosting to self-publishing, they are more likely to make more per copy of a book sold even though they miss out on an advance.

The amount a ghost can earn will vary wildly, but as a rule, the more bestsellers a ghost can lay claim to being involved with, the more they'll ask for to collaborate on the next one. For many ghosts, the most profitable way to work is to hedge their bets, doing a proportion of straight fee-based work, some on a guaranteed fifty fifty split and a small number of speculative projects that may or may not pay out significantly down the line. This takes some of the gamble out of the process, ensures the bills get paid and raises the prospect that one day soon a productive ghost will have a surprise bestseller on their hands. That way, next time around, they'll be able to secure one of those six figure advances.

In any ghosting fee arrangement, as with any business deal, the key is that all parties go into it with their eyes wide open. Skilled ghostwriting is often more expensive than people realise and it is worth exploring all the possibilities before agreeing to anything. Experienced ghosts are generally up front with authors when it comes to the financial side of things. Indeed, as Andrew Crofts says, he errs on the side of trying to explain to authors that penning a book is not always the path to riches.

I spend most of my time putting people off writing a book with me. I say: I guarantee it will be fun, you'll really enjoy doing it, but I cannot guarantee you will make money. You may have to look upon it as a very expensive hobby, rather like having a portrait painted. It should be a pleasure.

As soon as someone says; I need to make some money from my story, I say you won't make money if you hire a ghost because most times we charge more than you'll earn. If they are so sure it is going to be a bestseller, sometimes they go ahead anyway. Sometimes they win but most of the time they don't.

Usually people are pleased at the end, even if they get disappointments along the way. They may not get the publisher's bidding war, or all the things we all dream of, but normally they are pleased they have done it one way or another once they get used to the fact they have spent the money. At least their story will probably see the light of day, even if they don't get a publisher, thanks to print on demand. It doesn't always have to be a bestseller on the shelves in Waterstones. They can just print up 100 copies for friends and family and everyone will be very pleased to get it.

It is also worth noting that money isn't everything when ghosts are making up their minds to take on projects, whether it is on a fee-based arrangement, fifty fifty split or a tapered share of an advance. Yes, ghosts have bills to pay like everyone else and have to be convinced a project is financially viable, but another consideration that all ghosts take into account is the richness of the experience. While collaborating with an author is not a life-long commitment, spending three to six months or possibly even more getting close to someone and interpreting their story is quite an undertaking. No ghost wants to devote that much time to a person they either don't particularly like, or don't like spending time with. A sense of satisfaction and interest in the job is important to a ghost, particularly when they have their pick of projects. Ghosts variously describe how they feel 'more alive' when climbing into the lives of a perfect collaboration, or 'spoiled' by getting to hear first-hand the stories of the people they chose to collaborate with. Any author who wants to work with a ghost, particularly if they are asking them to work on spec, needs to find one who is as enthusiastic about their story as they are.

Some books are life changing for ghosts and not just financially. Author and ghost David Long spent more than two years working on a private chronicle for a well-known, yet highly secretive family and found it one of the most stimulating experiences of his life.

I lived with the family for three days, every two or three weeks, visiting all their houses, flying around in private planes and helicopters and being picked up and dropped off in chauffeured cars. It was complete emersion and unlike anything I had ever experienced before.

The first time I went there to interview them, I went on a scheduled airline. On the same plane, there were also two tutors, charming old Etonions, who were teaching the family's children through the holidays. When we got there, the butler was told the tutors were staying in a subsidiary house on the estate, but I belonged in the house with the family. Later on, I found out that the dogs had been flown up in the family jet, so that made me feel slightly less special. They sent their jet to pick up their dogs and us on a public carrier.

I occupied a strange space, I wasn't a servant, but I wasn't a supplier either. I was treated like a friend of the family. I would get home and send them a thank you note and their office an invoice for my time.

It was the best job I have ever done. It was completely extraordinary because I lived their life. At the end of it, after two and a half years, I found returning to my own life, not unsatisfactory, but at least bizarre because the contrast was so great.

Authors hoping to attract the attention of their chosen ghost don't have to offer private plane trips and chauffeured cars, but should think carefully about the best, most attractive, way to construct a deal for both parties. Ghost fee arrangements are as unpredictable as the rest of the publishing industry and flexibility is the key as the book business is always susceptible to fads and fashions.

CHAPTER FOUR
GHOST HUNTING, OR HOW TO FIND A GHOST

When any author starts looking for a ghost to work alongside them, there are many elements to consider, but how the two parties get along is paramount. Indeed, talk to ghostwriters about their relationship with named authors and vice versa and one word that comes up time and again is 'chemistry'. When a ghost and an author sign up to work together on a story, it is not the start of a life-long relationship, but it is certainly a commitment to a fairly intense, intimate process. If it is mismatched, rocky or strained from the beginning, by the time both parties get close to 80,000 words or so, it will be like being at the tail-end of a failed marriage. Very messy.

Working at achieving a smooth collaboration is important for a wide range of reasons, over and above pure chemistry. Another word bandied about a lot in ghosting is 'voice', as in 'finding the author's voice', or in other words projecting their personality through the written word. It stands to reason that if either party can't stand being in the same room as the other, the main author's voice is never destined to come across very well. Finding a good match is key to the success of any co-authored project.

To begin with, the onus is usually on the author to find the most suitable partner. After all, it is usually their name, expertise and/or fame that will sell the book. In the hunt for the perfect ghost, one of the easiest ways to ensure a good connection is to bring in someone already known to the author. It's quite common, for example, for celebrities to look-up a journalist who has previously written nice things about them in previous magazine or newspaper articles. The would-be author will be reassured that a), this person can string a sentence together, and b), they are probably going to toe the line. Plus, if the two parties have a previous connection, it makes a potential partnership a more attractive proposition for the ghost too, because they will know exactly what he or she is letting themselves in for. This can be essential in some collaborations, as Natalie Jerome, publisher at HarperCollins explains. Jerome commissioned and edited *Blessed*, the biography of legendary hard-drinking, hard-living, celebrity footballer George Best.

The chap who ghosted *Blessed* was a Telegraph journalist. George Best and he were good friends before they started work on the book and it was an obvious pairing. That is not to say it wasn't a challenging editorial experience for everyone concerned. George was quite unwell at the time and was under

an intense amount of media scrutiny for his drinking. It was important that the ghost was accommodating of these pressures.

Natalie Jerome does concede putting together these sorts of collaborations doesn't always go to plan unless everyone does their homework thoroughly.

I am very careful in the early selection process, because I want to avoid the awful moment where everyone realises it hasn't worked out. When candidates are shortlisted, I make sure there's an interview process. With careful planning, everyone knows what they are dealing with and what is expected of them.

I have had the experience where the personality was very comfortable with someone they respected and liked and I agreed to their recommendation, but when the text was submitted, I was disappointed. That's tricky to resolve so late in the day, and it reaffirms the importance of a publisher's role in choosing ghosts because, as well as looking for a harmonious ghost-author relationship, we're also aware of which ones will produce commercial material that will work in the market.

Unravelling a ghosting project that has gone sour is something that is often easier said than done and something all parties need to avoid. This is the main reason why the next ghost-hunting option is often the most unpopular. This is the scenario where an author enlists a friend with a flair for writing to help them with their book, even though the would-be writer may have little or no prior experience of penning anything longer than a brochure. There are obvious flaws to this strategy as Natalie Jerome has already pointed out and there is no doubt it is generally not the preferred option in the trade. Indeed, as Louise Dixon, senior editorial director Michael O'Mara Books says, it often makes her heart sink when well-known authors insist on bringing in a pal who 'fancies writing a book.'

If someone comes along with a 'friend who likes writing', it doesn't always work that well. It can do, but generally it is a job best left to professionals. I do take a deep breath when I hear a friend-of-a-friend is being brought in to help with a book.

One of the most common ways of organising a collaboration begins with a publisher or literary agent. Some literary agents have a number of ghosts on their books and, if the agent themselves are interested in a project, they can be very useful matchmakers lining up appropriate ghosts with authors who may benefit from their expertise. Jonathan Taylor, publishing director, at Headline Publishing estimates 50 per cent of the time a ghost will come to him as part of the package set up either by the author through prior links with the writer, or via a recommendation from a literary agent. The rest of the time he has an input into sourcing the co-writer. When he need to match-make a ghost with an author, his prime motivation is to find a ghost he 'knows and trusts' and who 'gets the tone and scope of the project'.

Most publishers have a pool of up to a dozen ghosts who they return to time and again. Most are pretty cagey about the writers they like because, as one admits, 'good ghosts are hard to come by'. They don't want to alert other publishers to the identity of this valued resource.

When it is obvious a ghost is required for a particular project, a publisher will usually get the ball rolling by setting up a beauty parade of three or more suitable writers for the author to meet. Very often this will take place at the publisher's head office, or, if the project is particularly shrouded in secrecy, at a secret location.

An author facing a line-up like this will have to consider the following practicalities when considering the ghost they'd like to work alongside:

Chemistry – Do they like each other? They have to be fully convinced that they will feel comfortable opening-up to this person, however difficult the subject matter.

Trust – Do they have complete faith that this person really knows what they are doing? An author has to be satisfied their ghost can produce a book that reflects what they've got to say and is a compelling read too.

Fun – Is the ghost going to be a good person to work with? It is not a lifetime commitment, but co-writers do need to spend a lot of time together, particularly in the early stages of collaboration. It will make a big, and potentially hugely damaging, difference if either party begins to dread the moment the other one walks through the door.

Experience - Most skilled writers can turn their hands to pretty much any subject, but it is helpful to delve into what they've done in the past. An author with a dramatic story that involves some sort of loss, might want to consider someone who has done misery memoirs in the past. If the author is a celebrity who is very glamorous or well connected, they may well seek out a ghost who is familiar with all the names they will be dropping.

Very often, authors will opt for a ghost who has a particular affinity or specialism in the subject in question. Ghostwriters, like actors, do tend to get typecast. A writer who has made a good fist of a business biography is probably a good bet to tackle another corporate blockbuster. Another who did well capturing the essence of the latest reality TV star, is probably going to be in line to take on the Next Big Thing on the small screen. It is a safe option and usually works out just fine.

However, as many publishers have found, the safe option doesn't always produce the most dynamic partnership, or indeed, the most compelling read. It doesn't always follow that thirty-something, young, female authors, should absolutely opt to collaborate with thirty-something, young female ghosts, or an older man will always work best with an older male ghost. Very often, as Weidenfeld & Nicolson's Alan Samson describes, the best, most creative, collaborations are between two people from vastly different backgrounds.

I have up to ten people in mind when I am looking for a ghost. The best ones are marvellous. They have an almost ventriloquial quality to become a Special Services soldier, an actress, a rock or sports star, or anyone else in the way they can capture the voice on a page. I often audition them, meaning that I invite three or four to come and meet the personality. What I am looking for is chemistry. I don't need to know whether they can write or not, since I already know their CVs are very impressive and diverse.

The results of these meetings are often counter-intuitive. I am not someone who puts opposites together in a Machiavellian way, but authors often naturally choose someone who is their opposite. An aristocrat wishing to pen their memoirs may get on better with the feisty, more challenging writer rather than choosing the immaculately well-mannered person I imagine they would prefer. A middle-aged female singing star might choose a ghostwriter who is a young person from a different field entirely. Opposites attract. Sometimes you just know from the beginning of a meeting they are going to get along like a house on fire. There is immediately a rapport.

It is a view shared by experienced ghosts too. According to Linda Barrett-Lee, who has ghosted books in many different genres, it is a mistake to always go for the 'obvious' ghost with an expertise in the author's particular area. Although the book will undoubtedly be technically brilliant, displaying a ghost's detailed knowledge and understanding of the subject, it may not be as effective at engaging people outside the immediate sphere of interest. Sometimes a wider range of skills is essential.

I adore Andy Murray. He is one of my sporting idols. He looks a lot like my own son and they have much the same attitude. I read some extracts of his biography and found it hard going though, so much so that I had to tell my family (who otherwise would have) not to buy it for me for Christmas. I think that's because I didn't get enough of a sense of Andy Murray the human being.

David Beckham's book, on the other hand, was a fantastic read, even though I am not remotely interested in football. I started reading the serialisation of his book in The Times and I couldn't wait for the next day's extract.

I don't know for sure, but I'd lay odds that Andrew Murray's book was written by a sports journalist, someone who was used to writing up sporting engagements. It really struck me how there seemed to be little story-telling going on. It was all about the tennis matches, but with very little in between. Beckham's book reads much more like a novel in the way it's pulled together as a story. I bet whoever co-wrote it has written some fiction.

As a rule, good ghosts are very versatile and are able to turn their hands to writing just about anything, however diverse. They have the skill of being able to absorb any subject and turn it into interesting prose. As a result, experienced ghosts are likely to have a wide range of different subjects in their portfolio.

Publishers admit they actively encourage this opposites-attract phenomenon, because it guarantees a fresh viewpoint to an author's story. HarperCollins' Natalie Jerome again:

The challenge for a publisher is how to present a familiar story in a fresh way, particularly when so much is already known about most celebrities. The key thing with a memoir is to bring something new and that means getting the author to open up, especially if they have been interviewed over and over again for newspapers, magazines and now for social media through the decades. If a publisher is not careful there can be a slight feeling of 'here we go again' when people pick up a book on a well-known personality. That is something we have to overcome. We have to make sure the memoir is engaging and saying something new, ideally heartfelt and honest.

This is often why someone from a different background is frequently well placed to get the best out of an author. They won't have a history together. For example, a music journalist might get a great story out of a boxer. The unfamiliar can work brilliantly.

A ghost's track-record in previous collaborations is an important consideration too. As we saw in chapter two, there are a number of internationally renowned and sought-after co-authors whose names actually add value to a book. There are only a handful of these big name ghosts, so competition to work with them is fierce. When it comes to creating commercially viable books, it's best not to scrimp on a ghost. As long as the chemistry is right, an author is advised to go for the best co-writer their advance will allow. A good ghost's input can transform a project, according to Weidenfeld & Nicolson's Alan Samson.

One particular example I would like to have published was *Always Managing*, the biography of football manager Harry Rednapp. He worked with Martin Samuel, from the Daily Mail, who is one of the finest football writers I know. Harry could have got a less talented football journalist, who would have packaged his excellent stories together adequately. In my view, though, the considerable success that this book had was in no small part due to Martin Samuel's writing. It is a truly interesting book, because as well as Harry being clearly knowledgeable, the shape and quality of the writing is excellent.

Sometimes there is no obvious choice of co writer, perhaps because the subject matter is not particularly mainstream and there are no experienced ghosts who appear to have expertise in the area. In this case, authors, agents and publishers may have to think creatively and pinpoint writers with specialist knowledge of a given area, even if they might not have previously considered ghosting. One of the most obvious points of call in this respect is journalists. For many writers, including Nadene Ghouri, this train of thought opens up a new career avenue and it becomes a neat introduction to the ghosting profession. Before she took up ghosting, Nadine had a background as a journalist and presenter.

I was approached out of the blue by a French publisher who had obviously Googled 'journalists writing about Afghanistan'. He asked if I would be interested in writing about Fawzia Koofi, a well known female MP, who is the only female presidential candidate in that country. I thought, that sounds interesting. I found out later that Fawzia had actually been through six writers before she came to me. The French publisher probably said to her; this journalist is your last chance.

They warned me she was a bit tricky and said I should give her a call to see how she felt about me. I called her and my first questions were designed to find out what she was about. I said; why do you do this? What makes you risk your life? She said; because of my daughters. I asked her; what is your greatest inspiration and she laughed and said; my mother.

Instantly I got her and realised this was a book about so much more than just Fawzia Koofi. It was about three generations of Afghan women. It was about her mother who was uneducated and one of six wives, an extraordinary MP and then her daughters who will probably end up going to Oxbridge, or Yale. I was able, in that first few minutes, to connect with Fawzia. She said later that I was the first writer who had called her and taken the time to do that.

There is quite a difference between journalism and ghosting. As a journalist I always had quite a limited interaction with the subjects of stories and then I walked away quite quickly once I had written my story. I rarely got to see the consequences of my story. As a ghost I get to spend weeks or months with my subject, getting them to reveal their inner most secrets. The level of responsibility is much, much bigger, but it gives a writer so much freedom too.

In Nadene's case there is clearly an element of choice. She was intrigued by Fawzia Koofi and wanted to devote some of her career to working with the MP. This, of course, brings us to ghosts themselves. While authors have the opportunity to choose their co-writers, it mustn't be forgotten that ghost's have an opinion too. Chemistry is, after all, a two way thing. Respected ghosts have the pick of high profile projects and many ghosts, not just big name ones, turn down many, many more potential collaborations than they accept. Ghosts are understandably cagey about the ones they reject, the secrecy goes with the territory, but US 'super ghost' Michael D'Orso has gone on record to say he has turned down several potential subjects over the years including Vice President Dan Quale, who he dubs 'an idiot' and pop star P. Diddy, dismissed as 'that asshole'.[6]

So once authors pinpoint the ghosts they'd like to work with, how do they catch their attention?

6   The Happy Ghost, Bill Morris, www.themillions.com

To begin with, just as publishers recoil from 'friends who fancy trying their hand at writing', ghosts are just as wary of wannabe authors who employ a co-writer because they feel they 'simply don't have the time' to pen their own book. The widespread view among professionals is this is a recipe for disaster. The author will almost certainly interfere, criticise and niggle all the way through and even if the pairing are still talking by the time the manuscript is complete, it is likely to turn out to be a complete dogs dinner. Writing by committee doesn't work, particularly if one party is so dogged in their approach, they refuse to listen to expert advice.

According to Lynne Barrett-Lee, the perfect pairing is when each party is left to get on with what they do best and fully respects one another's skills.

My favourite ghost subject is someone who says; I really love the story of my life and want to see it in a book, but I have no pretentions to being an author. When someone says this to me, it's music to my ears. There is no diplomatic minefield more dangerous than working with someone who thinks they are a writer of publishable standard when they're not. Professional writers have years of rejection under their belt, so have a nicely thickened skin. Most who work with a ghost haven't experienced this particular 'luxury', so can be understandably prickly when it's gently suggested the way they put things might be in need of improvement. In any event, I am always prepared for trouble.

I am also wary when the author has a partner who insists on getting too closely involved in the writing process. This has happened to me on a couple of projects I've worked on and usually it is most acute when the author I am working with has had a stab at writing their book and it is unpublishable for whatever reason. I'll be in a situation where I click with the author, who will be happy to trust my judgement, yet their other half can never get past the idea that their best beloved's work wasn't good enough as it stood. As soon as I start trying to take it back to first principles before putting it back together again, they can get very cross.

I had one situation in particular, where I wrote the raw material for an early chapter in outline, with the intention of going back to flesh it out later on. I put comment boxes in the margin with questions like; do you remember what this person was wearing? Or, do you remember what they sounded like? The person I was ghosting for was fine about it and happily answered all the questions. However, they also showed it to their partner. He broke in and said; well I think we should be doing this, or that, instead. Once anyone starts doing something like this my alarm bells start ringing. I went back to the author and explained that we had a problem: that we were in danger of having too many cooks, which might spoil the broth. She agreed and said she would stop sending the drafts to her partner. Things went much more smoothly after that.

Earlier on in my ghosting career I was a bit wishy washy about that sort of thing. I would probably have just moaned inwardly, and put up with it. It is a great joy to think I don't rely on any particular job these days, and can walk away from situations that aren't working out. Happily, though, it only happens rarely, as most people I've collaborated with have been delightful.

Sometimes, it has to be said, ghost and author get together by complete accident. Luckily the pairing just seems to gel and both parties are happy from the off. This was certainly the experience of Nicola Stow, who co-wrote *Born Gangster*, the biography of career gangster Jimmy Tippet Junior. The former News of the World journalist was out on a journalistic assignment alongside what she calls a 'gangster mad' photographer and one thing led to another.

We were waiting in the car outside some dodgy gangster's house in Glasgow and to kill the time I was talking about how I would like to write a book some day. The photographer said he knew a gangster who had had an interesting life who really wanted to do a book. I'm not sure I was even listening properly, but I said; what is his name? He said; Jimmy Tippet Junior. I said I had never heard of him, let me do my research before I agree to anything. Nah, he said, I'll give him a call. The next thing I know, Jimmy Tippet Junior is on the phone. He says: Alright darling, you gonna write my book then? A few days later I was

down in London meeting him. He had done a load of notes and was ready to go.

The basic rule any ghost would expect an author to adhere to is they bring the story and the ghost brings the writing expertise. As long as the author is better at talking than writing and is not a frustrated writer, the relationship should be just fine. An author also needs to understand and appreciate their collaborator will push them as far as they can go, even if it is sometimes feels uncomfortable. They have to be ready to answer everything, however painful. It is a leap of faith, on both sides, but if an author and ghost are careful to do their due diligence ahead of time, then the match will be good.

Chapter Five
What makes a good ghost?

One of the first questions ghostwriters usually get asked is how they feel about not getting the credit for their work.

'Doesn't it upset you that you don't get your name on the cover?' people ask with feigned concern when they get introduced to someone in the profession.

Of course, what most smart ghosts immediately answer is; as long as my name is on the cheque, it really doesn't matter. Ghostwriting is, after all, a job.

But, what makes a ghost good at that job? Let's take a top-notch aptitude in writing as a given for the moment. The answer to what makes a decent ghostwriter is: a great deal of very different skills.

Versitility is a key requirement, because a ghostwriter wears many hats. They may be writing a soap star's tell-all life story one month and move seamlessly to write a serious biography for a captain of industry the next. However, to be successful, a ghost also has to be able to create an almost instant rapport with all sorts of characters, many of whom come from some very different walks of life to their own. Plus, writing skills notwithstanding, any ghost worth their advance needs to know how to structure a compelling read out of what can very often be a 100,000 word stream of consciousness on an infinite range of subjects.

It's a balancing act which Nadene Ghouri, who ghosted international bestseller *The Favoured Daughter: One Woman's Fight to Lead Afghanistan into the Future*, calls 'part journalism, part therapy and part literary endeavour'.

It is a tricky balance of letting the author think they are in control, while you also need to get the job done. You must persuade them to tell you the most important dramatic, traumatic, upsetting things that have happened to them in absolute detail. Trust is a huge factor. If they don't have faith that you will tell their story accurately and with sensitivity, you may as well forget it.

Then, once you've got the story recorded, you have to bring it to life on the page. I can only describe it as being a bit like being a literary method actor. One has to get inside a person's head and hear not only the most powerful or emotional aspects of their factual story, but you also have to listen to the rhythm of their voice, the quirks and characteristics, the way of speaking that makes that person them.

There are many similarities between ghostwriting and acting. When ghosts write for someone else, many do try to almost become that person. It is a real asset to see what they saw, feel what they felt and know what they learned. It's what brings a story to life.

Interestingly though, the profession that has become most closely aligned with ghostwriting in recent years is journalism.

There are also a great many similarities between the skills needed to ghost a book successfully and those that make an effective journalist. Journalists are expected to meet people they know virtually nothing about, or certainly who they have never met before and quickly win their trust. In the space of a few hours, or even less, they need to get a subject to open up and tell them the most salient parts of their story, however painful it may be and then find a way to present it in the most compelling and easy-to-understand way. This experience makes a perfect grounding for a career in ghostwriting.

Journalistic experience in independent research is also an essential skill. In chapter eight we cover the practicalities of interviewing but the fact is, not all the information for a book will necessarily come from the author. For various reasons a ghost will often have to bring a lot of their own material to the party. Tim Tate, a TV documentary producer who worked with investigative journalist Roger Cook on the TV show The Cook Report, found the skills honed on the programme came in handy on his collaboration with Sarah Forsyth for the book *Slave Girl*.

In 2007 I worked with Roger Cook on his valedictory documentary which re-examined his most successful investigations. One of those investigations was the story of Sarah Forsyth who was trafficked

from Gateshead to Amsterdam. She was fed crack cocaine and cannabis and forced at gunpoint to work as a prostitute. Ten years on we tracked her down as part of a wider investigation into modern sex trafficking. John Blake bought the rights to her story and we wrote it together.

Sarah had clearly been to hell and back and was still in hell when I first started interviewing her. She'd spent a long time in the windows of Amsterdam's red light district, had become addicted to crack and was an alcoholic too. Although she was now off the drugs, she was still taking methadone and inevitably there were a number of gaps in her memory. There were some incidences she remembered very vividly, but many were told through the eyes of someone who was in a haze of pain and drugs.

A writer can't use their imagination to fill in the gaps on a story like that. It is too important to be imagined. Fortunately, I had done enough films about the sex trade in Amsterdam, so I knew the location. I tracked down the police who handled her case in the UK and Holland and spoke to her family. I did an awful lot of journalistic research.

Clearly, the speed at which trained journalists are used to working is also huge asset in ghosting a product which is destined for commercial use. Many first time authors will tell stories of the months and years they spend agonising over each paragraph, meaning some books take an age to be completed, if at all. Yet, if a book doesn't make it into the shops, it clearly won't pay its way. Conversely, a journalist-turned-ghostwriter will interview a subject, gather any additional research and knock the result into shape in a fraction of that time. It's what they do.

Shannon Kyle, is a case in point. A journalist from the Sunday People and Take-A-Break, she wrote Jade Goody's autobiography *Jade: Forever in my heart*, in the reality TV star's final weeks before her untimely death from cancer. After accepting the assignment, Shannon had less than three weeks to interview both the star and her family and turn the transcripts into a finished manuscript.

I worked manically day and night. I spent a lot of time at Jade's house talking to her husband and her mum and even spent a weekend with her bridesmaids from her earlier wedding to Jack Tweed. It was only at the end that I finally crashed and had time to think about just how sad it all was.

Like journalists, ghostwriters also need to be confident by nature, because they will frequently have to ask some awkward questions. After all, no one can worm their way into an author's innermost, intimate thoughts and mine their memories without a little chutzpah now and again.

It is for this reason that Alan Samson, publisher at Weidenfeld & Nicolson, says former tabloid journalists often make particularly effective ghosts.

The new breed of modern ghosts have to be able to ask searching personal questions, sometimes be as bold as brass, and of course be able to write. These

multiple qualities are what many tabloid journalists possess, and that is why they can add value to a book project.

This is not to say that only journalists made good ghosts. Indeed, many accomplished ghosts don't have a newsgathering background at all. Lynne Barrett-Lee, the ghost behind several bestsellers such as *Never Say Die, The Girl with No Name* and *Mum's Way*, has a background as a novelist.

Ghostwriting is first and foremost about story-telling to me. It is about taking a series of events and turning it into a narrative. To me that is a completely different discipline to journalism.

Whatever their background, to get this narrative ghosts do need to have the personality and presence to get close to their subjects. While many writers might take up the profession because they enjoy the solitary aspect of the job spending long hours alone in front of a computer, it doesn't mean they can freeze when they get out into the real world. There is no room for shyness in ghosting.

It's a big plus if a ghostwriter is naturally interested in people and confident in their own abilities. The more inquisitive they are, the more comprehensive and insightful the finished product is likely to be. To do this Lynne Barrett-Lee says ghosts need to be 'upfront, assertive and audacious' in their questioning.

Don't be shy about getting personal – ghost-writing is personal. So ask the sensitive, squirmy,

questions you know the reader will be asking. That way you can pre-empt them and hopefully address them.

Good interviewers do more than just ask the right questions too. They look around and gather rich detail about their client with their eyes. That's why most ghosts prefer to do their interviewing in an author's home, or another place that is of great importance to the subject. It is possible to learn a whole lot about a person by seeing details such as where they place their TV, whether they display antique encyclopaedias, or cricket trophies and how they interact with those closest to them.

It's what ghostwriter Katy Weitz calls 'full immersion'.

I root around a subjects home, get close, sniff around their fridge, meet their mother, look at their photos. You have to be them so you have to know them inside out. I really need that full immersion.

Experienced ghostwriters spend time getting to know every detail of an author's background. This might mean researching the area where they were brought up and popular styles in fashion and music during their formative years. Some ghosts have even gone as far as moving in with their subject to become part of the family for a while.

Little things are important here, such as commonly used terms, phrases or cultural trends that shaped the time and even the political environment, if applicable. Being thorough in this way is an intensive and time consuming process, but it is all part of the mix. Often an author might not necessarily believe this detail to be important, but it will stand out a mile if a ghost glosses over it.

Staying tactful under the occasional trying situation is most definitely the lot of a ghost. It's a character trait that's closely aligned with empathy and as any ghost will tell you, you won't get anywhere unless you can get your interviewee to trust you. That means the subject has to truly believe there is some understanding of their story before they completely open up. An interviewer has to show genuine empathy.

Although a good rapport has to be gained almost immediately, trust is something that is built up over time as the author responds to the empathy of his or her ghost. To achieve this, a ghost has to work at making their subject feel completely comfortable. In fact, they need to become their champion. Yes, even after the author's biggest mistakes and most unpleasant personality traits are laid bare, a ghost must *believe in* the person they are working with. That's not to say that if the subject is, say, an international crime lord, the ghostwriter has to necessarily condone his or her choice of career, but simply that they understand and accept them for what they've done, warts and all.

Andrew Crofts, one of the UK's best-known ghostwriters, who has written dozens of international bestsellers, says a ghost who criticises, argues, or appears to judge a subject, dooms the collaboration from the beginning.

If the author feels judged, they will never relax, open up or talk honestly. It's not a ghost's job to try to make them change their opinions about anything or anyone, but rather to encourage them to tell their story in the most interesting and coherent way possible.

Returning to the acting theme mentioned earlier by Nadene Ghouri, one way around any concerns over the morality of a subject, is for a ghost to find a way to get into character. One ghost, who has helped a number of subjects in the criminal fraternity to write books, says he draws inspiration by watching re-runs of the classic 70s police TV drama The Sweeney. Nicola Stow on the other hand, who collaborated with Jimmy Tippett Junior, a career gangster, said that while many of her author's tales were gritty and rich in violence, his irrepressible humour and unpredictability made all the difference.

A lot of the process was quite farcical really. He had a different mobile phone SIM card every day and you could only ever get him for ten minutes at a time. He'd promise to call back in five minutes and then would disappear for two days. When you did get him though, he was a real motor mouth and a brilliant character.

It's not always as easy for a ghost to cut a path through the unruly jungle of anecdotes. Generally, the longer a person has been in the public eye, the more likely they are to turn to the tired stories that have sustained their career. Naturally, if the story has been aired a few times, they may seek to spice it up by embellishing it with a few new details which is where things can start to get out of hand if a ghost isn't on top of their brief. A competent ghost will find a way to encourage the author out of their comfort zone and cut through the easy laughs to find out what it is that makes that person who they really are.

To pull off what can sometimes be a deep intrusion into an author's life, there is another vital skill that no ghost can do without: people skills. A ghost needs to be pleasant to work with, or, as one ghost-writer put it; be more 'Casper' than 'poltergeist'. It is not always easy because some authors are not at all sure they want to be paired with a ghost, explains ghostwriter Caro Handley. In circumstances like this the hostility from one side can make building up trust a real challenge.

Over the years I have gained a reputation for being good at working with people who are hard to deal with. An editorial assistant at Hodder & Stoughton routed out a book from the slush pile called *Gypsy Boy* by Mikey Walsh and thought there was something in it. She put him together with one ghost and it didn't work out well, so they bought me in. I very quickly realised that the problem was that Mikey was terrified that the book would be taken out of his hands. He thought that if he started to work with a ghost, he would lose control of his story completely and he

would have no say over it at all. He was very wary and defensive.

At times like this, all you can do is work hard to build up trust and win him over. It helped that I could see from the original manuscript that he had a real touch for black humour and a raw edge I really didn't want to lose. Once he understood that I could see that and that I was going to consult him at every stage, he began to relax.

Fundamentally a ghost's job can be very taxing, time consuming and emotionally draining, but any stress or anger as a result of the process can never be passed on to a client. No one wants to be around someone who argues with them all the time and that goes doubly so when one party is revealing their deepest secrets. People will only work with ghosts they enjoy being with and like. It's not going to be smiles and laughs all the way, particularly if challenging material is on the agenda, but it makes a big difference if an author is happy to spend time with their ghost, rather than dreading the moment they walk through the door.

One of the biggest advantages of these people skills is they contribute greatly to the process of finding an author's voice, because they help a ghost get closer to the author and intuitively feel their emotions and perceptions.

Flexibility and patience are two more attributes that should rank very highly in a ghostwriter's repertoire. Ghosts need to be able to operate around an author's schedule, and to do this, they'll need an infinite supply of patience. It's quite common for subjects, whether they are big named stars, or busy businessmen, or simply nervous individuals, to simply not turn up to arranged interviews. Or to cancel them at a drop of a hat. Or to bring along a whole bunch of their closest friends to 'give their input', which is exactly what a ghost doesn't need.

One ghost, let's call him Philip, tells of several aborted meetings with a subject, a household-name comedian. Then, one day, he arrived at his apartment and found to his surprise and pleasure, the man was dressed, sober and raring to go. There was no one in the house and even the dog had been taken out for a walk. They'd been talking for ten minutes when the phone rang. It transpired the comedian was supposed to be on his way to a public appearance 400 miles away in Glasgow. Guess where Philip ended up that day?

Meanwhile, however maddening it is to bend to the author's schedule, whether it is social or business-led, a ghost cannot allow themselves to be distracted by other considerations. The role of a ghost is to be 100 per cent focussed on the project in hand.

While many professional authors will take on ghosting projects to generate income while they work simultaneously on what they hope will be their next bestseller, the most effective ghosting collaborations generally come about when a ghost dedicates their whole mind to the writing project. It is very difficult to clear your head and start thinking like someone else when you are wearing many different hats each day.

Finally, it is worth noting, the attribute ghosts need the least is an ego. If a ghostwriter yearns for the pleasure and delight of seeing their names on the cover when they wander through Waterstones then they are undoubtedly in the wrong profession. Jokes aside about names on cheques, this is fortunately one accomplishment that bothers the majority of ghosts the least. Indeed, Ingrid Connell, editorial director at Sidgwick & Jackson, notes among the new generation of ghosts, there is noticeably less concern over public acclaim.

In my experience at least, there are a lot of ghosts today who are very pragmatic about this, who just want to keep working and might write as many as three books a year. But they still care very much about the quality of the book.

It's certainly easier and a great deal more pleasurable for a ghost to walk away at the end of one project and move straight on to the next. Once their job is done, it is over to the author to play their part in earning their advance. They have to get involved in an endless and gruelling round of marketing, PR appearances and promotional opportunities. It is, after all, the author's book, both in their own eyes and in those of their readers.

Also, not having a name emblazoned on the cover can actually be a plus point for a ghost. It is the perfect way to keep them one step removed from the process, so they can take a dispassionate and objective view of the story and present it in the best, most entertaining light.

Luckily, for most ghosts, the pleasure comes from doing a job they love and getting paid for it. Add to that the fact they get the opportunity to meet some extraordinary people and ask them anything they fancy and you can see the arrangement isn't bad for either party.

CHAPTER SIX
HOW TO BECOME A GHOSTWRITER

Like countless other ghost writers, I am an accidental ghost. An accidental ghost is someone who is happily involved in another career, in my case journalism, when someone comes along with an offer that can't be refused. I was contacted by Allan Leighton, the former boss of the Royal Mail, Selfridges and Asda Wall-Mart, among other blue chip businesses. I had interviewed him several times in the past for articles and we got on well. When he was signed up by Random House to pen his book *On Leadership* and needed a writer he trusted to help him, he gave me a call.

When Allan first raised the idea, I had never considered writing a book. Indeed, as I was fond of saying, I believed I was one of the few journalists in the world who didn't actually have a book in them. Up until then, I was more used to writing 500 word news stories and features, not 80,000 word books. I've always liked a challenge though and thus my ghost writing career was born.

Although journalism is one of the most obvious routes in, ghosts can come from a variety of often completely unconnected professions. Ghost writer Emma Murray began her career in marketing for an investment banking house.

I was writing about a lot of financial stuff which didn't exactly thrill me, so I decided to throw my hat into the ring and see if I could do something more interesting with my writing. I was a little wary about becoming a freelance writer because I didn't have any work to show for myself, so I started as an editor and proof-reader.

I worked hard to make connections, going to book fairs and joining The Society of Young Publishers (SYP), taking any opportunity I could get. One small publisher hired me to write an introduction for a book on care homes which was easily the most boring job I had ever had in my whole life. The money wasn't so great either. At one stage I even toyed with turning it down. I am glad I didn't because the editor who hired me ended up moving to Wiley-Capstone. She got in touch with me out of the blue to see if I would like to do a book on Alan Sugar. I wrote it in three months and it went to number one in the WHSmith business chart. It was a real feather in my cap and did wonders for my reputation. After that I started to get a lot more work as an author and ghostwriter.

Tom Watt came into writing after a varied career as an actor on TV soap Eastenders and radio sports presenter. His view is it is not background or career experience that is important. The most essential attributes to be a good ghost is having the right pre-disposition.

You need to enjoy listening to other people's stories. That is important. You also need the ability to give yourself over to another person. It works in much the same way as when an actor gives themselves over to a character. A ghost doesn't just tell the story. They tell it in a voice that is recognisably the author's voice rather than a flat one that could belong to virtually anyone.

When I am collaborating on a book, I find I go to almost completely the same place in my head as when I am acting. It is like acting in reverse. Rather than starting with a script and bringing it to life, you have got the life and you are turning it into a script.

I've never classified myself as a ghost. I just help other people tell their stories.

Ghost writing is now becoming a career of choice for many people from all walks of life who quite rightly see it as a legitimate, and rewarding, route to make money out of writing. So how is it possible to break into the profession?

Firstly a few observations of the most well-trodden routes into the business:

-   Most ghosts have already established them-selves in a career as a writer, often as a jour-nalist or a copywriter.

- Another route is to be an authority in a particular area. Say someone is an expert in food and nutrition; they could promote themself as a specialist ghost writer for diet and health books.
- A great way to show your credentials as a would-be ghost is to get published under your own name. In the past, this was not the easiest task, but now there are lots of opportunities to self publish a book, or series of books. For a ghost writer, this can be a powerful calling card.

Most people honing in on a career as a ghost writer would probably guess the number one skill needed for a successful career in collaboration is 'being a good writer'. While being able to write well is vital, it makes up a surprisingly small percentage of the qualities needed to become a success in this business. In fact, take good writing as a given. It takes a special sort of writer to be a successful ghost. In the previous chapter we talked about essential skills for a good ghost, such finding an author's voice and presenting it on the page, plus how vital good structure and pace is to the end product. Then there are all important interview techniques that help a ghost in getting an author to feel comfortable enough to tell all. However, to make a living as a ghost, there are loads of additional talents required.

Most important for anyone wanting to earn a decent living as a co-writer is the requirement to be pretty business savvy. The key word here is 'decent', because ghosting can be a very profitable profession. For an industrious, creative, practical and energetic ghostwriter it is possible to earn a very good living indeed. Although there are only a handful of ghosts that boast a significant share of million pound, or dollar, advances, there is also a second tier of hugely successful, jobbing, ghosts who take home respectable six figure salaries each year. However, to achieve anything like this level, ghosts can't think of themselves as mere writers for hire. They are entrepreneurs running a ghostwriting firm and that means investing time in building up a presence, networking with a steady supply of viable prospects and constantly presenting a corporate face. Working out a way to get a good, steady, stream of paying clients and being prepared to do some hard negotiation to get the deal they want with those clients are the business tools that are key to survival.

If a ghost doesn't have this business acumen, they will soon become unstuck and very broke indeed. Writing a book is no small undertaking and usually takes many months. It doesn't make any sense for a ghost to quote a rock bottom price just to get the gig. That is the money the ghost will be living off for weeks to come. Ghosts have to be very clear on their terms and prepared to press their case home, or walk away if necessary. There will always be pressure to work for free. Indeed, as all established ghosts discover, as they become better known they will get regular approaches from hopeful authors who are convinced they will make a bundle of money from their potential bestseller. However, if they have no money to pay or are unwilling to consider a fair split of any profits it is not worth considering. One regular ghost, Clive, explains the routine.

'They give the barest explanation of the details, or worse still refuse to divulge the details at all, in case I nick the idea. They breathlessly say, everyone tells me I should write it, I know it will sell like hot cakes. The expectation is I will do a dance of joy and immediately take on the task. What they don't seem to get is it could take six months of my time and there is no guarantee of any money whatsoever.

'My favourite was one lady who I had never met before, who finished by asking if I would consider doing it as a favour. It was like I don't need to pay my rent, or feed the family.'

Ghosts need to think like an entrepreneur because getting good quality leads to meet prospective authors is one of the hardest aspects of being a ghost. How do co-writers let people know they are ready, willing and supremely qualified to write their books to begin with? After all, the irony of ghosting is the ghost is supposed to be invisible, but if this is the case how is it possible for them to show off their wares? Ghosts have, over the years, found a variety of solutions to the problem. One of the most difficult, yet potentially most lucrative, is to impress a publisher and to get put on their list of recommended ghosts. That way, when there is a beauty parade of co-writers invited in to meet an author, the favoured few will usually get an invitation. It is then up to them to impress the author to get in on the deal.

Another technique is to alert authors via an advert. Andrew Crofts was one of the first ghost writers to do this when, at the beginning of his career, he began taking out a regular small ad in the industry bible The Bookseller. These days a number of ghosts advertise online via services such as Google AdWords. Ghosts are also turning to author's agents such as Andrew Lownie, Diane Banks Associates and Curtis Brown, who have built up a stable of ghosts on their books. The system works well for both sides. It gives ghosts a chance to pitch for a variety of work and agents get access to a good supply of ghosts on tap who they can readily pair with inexperienced writers.

However, it is worth noting, many agents like to keep the number of ghosts they work with to a manageable figure. As Diane Banks says, there is a finite amount of work to go around.

We get approached by a lot of would-be ghosts, but we do keep our numbers pretty tight. There is only so much ghosting work out there and if we take on too many we'll be making promises we can't keep. We aim to keep a balanced stable of writers, a mix of male and female, of different ages with differing interests. If a publisher comes to us with a project, we usually have a fit for them.

The main skill we look for is the ability to interview, rather than the ability to write per se. We do get novelists who fancy ghosting, but while they may be able to write, what you don't know is how good they are at getting into someone's head, or winning their trust. Most of our ghosts tend to be former journalists because it is a directly transferable skill.

If you build a reputation you will regularly be in work. Publishers will ask specifically for well-known ghosts. Getting there in the first place is quite tricky. It is quite a risk for a publisher to hire a ghostwriter who has never written a book before. We try to keep the list carefully and deliberately curated and trade off on the fact our ghosts are top quality, have a strong track record and will deliver.

As Diane says, there is little value in a would-be ghost advertising themself as a writer for hire if they have had no experience and nothing to show potential clients. Experience is really important in ghosting because authors need to feel comfortable that their co-writer is bringing considerable expertise to the party.

In the beginning writers may have to take a few very low paid, or even no paid, ghosting jobs, to help build up a portfolio of work. Would-be ghosts could start out by asking people they know if they want to collaborate on writing a book. Or, perhaps, persuading people they know to introduce them to people they know. Sometimes, if there are no obvious candidates, the only answer is to keep an ear to the ground and listen out for anyone with an extraordinary story to tell. Alternatively, new ghosts may even consider bidding for jobs on sites like guru.com. The money will be terrible, but it will help them build up some references for their work as a freelance.

It doesn't have to be full book collaborations either. Madeleine Morel, who runs a New York agency specialising in ghost writers, says would-be ghosts should be prepared to do anything to get their name seen.

Get your by-line out there in as many places as possible, be it magazines, books, blogs or one-liners. See which agents are selling the type of books you want to write and contact them. Approach the smaller publishing houses, the ones that will pay $5.000 to write a 100,000-word book on the 'Idiots Guide to…' At least then you'll be able to say you've written something.

Once ghosts do have some experience under their belt, they need to be proactive in promoting themselves. A website is essential and it should include some examples of work and perhaps some samples and testimonials from satisfied clients. Ghosts might also give some thought to building up an online presence on social media such as Twitter and Facebook, as well as via a blog. Word of mouth is a powerful tool too, so happy clients should always be asked to make a recommendation to any people they know.

Ghosts should also bear in mind, there is more to finding the right co-writer than the fact they are able to pay the bill, or willing give a decent cut of the profits. While authors often like to interview a beauty parade of ghosts, ghosts also need to be choosy when it comes to their clients, even at the early stage of their career. It is a useful skill to be able to sum up, very quickly, whether the person you are speaking to is someone you'd like to work with and their subject is something you'd genuinely like to write about. As any ghost will tell you: if you are not particularly gripped at the initial meeting, you'll be bored rigid long before you've ploughed through an 80,000 word manuscript.

The handful of questions a ghost should ask a prospective co-writer should include:

What kind of book do they want to write?

Who do they see reading the book? (And why will the reader particularly seek out their take on the subject?)

Why do they want to write their book?

Have they tried writing it themselves? If so, is it possible to see a sample of material?

Have they thought through, or even understood, the variety of publishing options and, if so, when were they hoping to see it published?

Do they have a budget for the project, or some ideas on how they see the fees being split?

Ghosts should listen carefully to the responses, because they will need to decide quickly whether the person they are speaking with is someone they can work with, or whether to pass. While chemistry is important, practical considerations such as whether the project is viable for both parties and indeed the book-buying public, are key.

Once a ghost begins to establish their career and work does begin to come in, the business savvy comes into play once again. In order to make a lucrative living, they need a steady flow of work. It plays havoc with personal cash flow to have huge gaps between the end of one project and the beginning of the next one. In an ideal world, a ghost will finish one book and move almost seamlessly onto the next one and that is what an entrepreneurial ghost needs to aim for. This means while they are penning a book, they need to not just have an eye to the next project, they should be actively pursuing it.

Juggling a couple of projects is not as tricky as it first sounds. A ghost could, for example, be finishing the edits on one book, while beginning the interviews for the next project and perhaps having 'toe in the water' discussions about the one after that. While it is virtually impossible to write two books at the same time, there is nothing stopping a ghost pushing other projects on in either the early or late stages. In fact, it makes good business sense.

Strong management skills clearly make a huge difference here. OK, it doesn't quite fit everyone's image of a tortured writer penning a novel in a garret, but a ghost with a strong track record of managing projects and deadlines, who is good at organising large amounts of research and juggling deadlines, will get a steady stream of good work.

Similarly, another business-style talent that will help a ghost naturally rise above their competitors is to be able to demonstrate a good understanding of their industry. There are massive changes in the publishing world and the bar is being raised ever higher by the major publishing houses. Meanwhile, there are several new publishing options and there is no doubt the democratisation of the market will continue to increase opportunities for online and self publishing. There are many variables which are baffling to people outside the industry, so a ghost has an opportunity to step in and confidently help authors weigh up the right options for them. There is nothing better to put an inexperienced author at ease than giving them valuable advice about the various directions they might choose.

Ghosts at an early stage in their career, may like to give some thought as to whether they are going to focus on any particular area. Although ghosts are pretty flexible and might turn their attention to anything from a celebrity biography, to a misery memoir, it occasionally pays to specialise. If, for example, a ghost already has an expertise in a particular area, they might use it as a unique selling point. A former sports journalist may tackle one sporting hero after another, while someone who has always been steeped in the corporate world might be ideal to communicate the thoughts of various captains of industry.

Tom Watt, for example, specialises in books about football because he is passionate about the sport and focussed his energies on forging a career writing and speaking about it.

It is what I am into and know about. My first book *The End: 80 Years of Life on the Terraces* was a labour of love. It was written at the time of the Taylor Report, when all the terraces at football grounds were disappearing. I decided to do an oral history of Arsenal's North Bank. I felt there was a story to be told because an awful lot had happened on those terraces that had never been committed to paper. Most of it had happened to people who didn't have the wherewithal, the wish, or the need to tell their stories. I worked from interviews to tell the stories of the generations of supporters, families, heroes and villains who had spent their Saturday afternoons together since the First World War.

Since then I have written, among other things, books on English football, an official history of Wembley Stadium and *Oscar's Brazil* with the Chelsea player Oscar to coincide with the 2014 World Cup.

Ghost writers don't just have to stick to non-fiction either. There are plenty of opportunities to ghost fiction too. Plus, they don't even need to stick with books at all. While this book has primarily dealt with books, the avenues in this profession include short stories, speeches, corporate material, educational manuals, blogs and even tweets.

If all this sounds like a lot of hard work, it might be worth thinking about the upsides to being a ghost writer. The first, and most obvious, is the opportunity to write and be paid for it. Also, while a ghost can help advise an author on the market and the various options available, they won't ever have to carry the marketing load. In other words, they won't ever have to attend a gruelling book signing tour, or drag themselves off to a local radio interview, or submit themselves to a lengthy Q and A session with a succession of special interest magazines.

A career as a ghost is perfect for anyone who enjoys their privacy and anonymity, not to mention solitude. Plus, for a person that relishes a challenge, ghosting is a real opportunity. A ghost writer will constantly be stretched because they have to get to know a subject as well as an author, better even, and present it in a readable way. Right now, for example, you might think you know all about dieting. You may even attempt one every New Year. Yet, if you are the ghost who is signed-up to collaborate with a well known dieting authority on their latest book, you will have to learn about human psychology and physiology, food groups, nutritional therapies and trends, health policies and statistics, and so on. It is quite likely the ghost-diet-guru will have to dig through volumes of research, interview various experts and will even end up being a bit of an expert themselves. Interestingly though, that will be just one field in which they have expert knowledge. After a few years in the profession, a ghost will know about dozens of subjects. They will also be called upon to write about subjects they may previously have known nothing about whatsoever.

Ghosting also offers all the advantages of any entrepreneurial venture, such as the satisfaction of being your own boss, as well as a bit of added flexibility thrown in. Don't want to work today? Fine, catch up tonight, or at the weekend, or whenever it feels right. As long as the manuscript is delivered on deadline, a ghost can make their own schedule.

Being disciplined and having some sort of routine is essential though and most ghosts set a daily or weekly word target. Alternatively, as Emma Murray does, a ghost may set themselves a goal to complete a chapter every two weeks.

I work part-time and have figured out from experience how long it takes me to write a chapter of 10,000 to 12,000 words and aim to do up to 2000 words a day to be safe. I am quite structured, but not as structured as other ghosts I know. I have a friend who practically has spread sheets to organise her writing schedule.

Neil Simpson, whose daily word target depends on the project and deadline, says once he sets the goal in his mind, he will not stop writing until he reaches it.

If I am on a tight deadline and I know I just have to do 4000 words a day, every day, I know I can't get up and leave my desk until they are done. I have to do that 4000. I might have to go back and change them

tomorrow, but I have to do it or tomorrow I will have to do 5000 or 6000 to make up for the ones I have missed the day before. I hate falling behind. It scares me to the pit of my stomach the thought of falling behind, so I just get on with it.

I do admit that the minute I get to 4001 I will literally switch off my computer and leave the room.

Of course, ghosting also has all the disadvantages of an entrepreneurial enterprise too. As detailed earlier in the chapter, there are no certainties to getting work and, without careful management, there can be long and worrying dry periods. When there is work, a ghost will also suffer the same downside as any homeworker. The work will always be there, teasing, pleading or scolding, wanting attention. It takes discipline not to nip into the study to dash out a couple of hundred words when you suddenly gain inspiration after a family day out. Plus, as every homeworker knows, it can be quite lonely, even for someone who is quite self sufficient. Named authors will, at least, get a flurry of social activity around book launch time, but for ghosts the invisibility is there week after week. Quite often, the only person they'll see professionally is their agent or the author they are working with and even then it will only be for a handful of hours. It is possible to combat this isolation by actively building up a strong support network and, indeed, it is a sensible move to get out and start networking because very often a ghost never knows where their next job will come from.

As discussed earlier, anyone with an ego shouldn't even consider ghosting as a career, because being fine about taking a back seat is a big part of the profession. This lack of ego will also come into play when ghosts tell people what they do for a living. After the astonished gasp and the question, don't you mind someone else taking credit for your work, people will often want to know why you don't want to write books under your own name? Or, as one interviewer asked a ghost who had upwards of twenty books under her belt; don't you want to be a *proper* writer?

There are a number of answers to this question. In truth, many ghosts do hanker after a career as a novelist. Indeed, a number of ghosts have successfully published under their own name, Fanny Blake, Lynne Barrett-Lee and Andrew Crofts to name but a few and the two careers can compliment each other beautifully. However, as any writer knows, the publishing world is a tough place to be, and increasingly so. Publishing advances are hard to come by and are often far lower than the fees that can be gained from ghost writing. It is very hard to make a living as an author these days. A tiny percentage of authors actually do. It is, for this very reason, many established authors are crossing to the ghosting side. Sometimes family security is more important than fulfilling a wish to see a name in lights.

Increasingly though, ghostwriting is being recognized as an enjoyable, varied and fulfilling career in its own right. Indeed, there are many advantages to ghosting, over and above the fact it presents an opportunity to make money out of writing. Ghosts are given the opportunity to dip in and out of the most amazing stories about people's lives. Established ghosts can write up to three or four books a year and be in constant work.

Chapter Seven
Getting Started
on a Collaboration

In any biography, or work of non-fiction, it is easy for a first-time author to think the story itself is enough. After all, it is what happened isn't it? In truth though, the story is never enough. Indeed, believe it or not, it is actually a very small part of what will make a book a success. Non-fiction is not the truth. It is an edited, dramatised, souped-up version of the truth that carefully selects key aspects of a story and discards other, less interesting, bits. Sorting out the most powerful story is what a ghost does best.

Ghosts are invaluable in guiding authors to think more deeply about plot lines and characterisation because, even though real life events are being recorded, it is the way they are told that will bring a book alive. No reader wants a 100 per cent accurate, blow-by-blow account of someone's life story, however much of a die-hard fan they are of the person in question. They want to be entertained and they want the person they are reading about to come alive, warts and all, in the most arresting way possible. That means they don't need to know every single detail from their school grades to their medical records, unless of course it is relevant to the bigger picture. It is a ghost's job to pick out the most important parts of the story and present them in the most compelling way.

This is not a license to lie, but it is an invitation to occasionally stretch the truth a little when necessary and certainly to leave out superfluous detail that would only ever be interesting to close family, if at all.

It is for this reason that, once a ghost has been chosen and the chemistry checked, the first part of the ghosting process has to be to nail down the nuts and bolts of what the book will cover. The most efficient way to do this is for the ghost to map out a chapter-by-chapter plan following a one-to-one interview with the author. During this interview, the author will be asked to summarise their story and the key elements they see as most relevant. A ghost won't expect an exhaustively detailed account, but does need some idea of names, dates and significant events. The real detail can be added later. The elements gathered at this initial briefing are vital to construct a meaningful plan.

There are established authors such as Stephen King who argue a plan stifles the creative process, but in a two-way collaboration there really is no other way. Although in this early stage, after an author spends just a few hours with their ghost, it is impossible to uncover all the gems hidden in an author's head, it gives both parties a guide to the direction the book may take. It'll give the ghost an idea of the most powerful way to structure the book and the author an idea of the areas of his or her life that are deemed the most interesting by the professional writer.

This process will also set the shape, or structure of the book, which is the glue that holds it together. If everyone agrees on the core theme, or foundation, of the story, it will prove invaluable in keeping a book on track. If, for example, the celebrity author is an actor and decides half way through relating his life story of triumph against movie business sharks he would actually rather talk at length about his love of rare orchids, the ghost will be able to gently push him back around to what was agreed in the plan following the initial interview. With structure, things can go a bit awry, but they will never go too far wrong. If any parts of the story in subsequent author interviews are pointless, or don't add anything, they will stand out a mile.

Occasionally, as Tom Watt explains, a ghost may set themselves ground rules on the background research they do before they start interviewing an author. Tom ghosted David Beckham's biography *Beckham*.

Ground rule number one was I didn't consult any newspaper cuttings. If I used the cuttings, I'd just be getting David's reactions to what the papers said about him which was rubbish. The only desk research I did was via Manchester United's database and the very good England fan's one. The actual detail for

dates, games and the rest of the story I got from talking to his mum and dad, Victoria, Gary Neville and the people involved with David at the time the story was happening.

You ask anyone what they were doing on a particular day 20 years ago and they probably wouldn't have a clue. If, though, you can remind them what the occasion was - and it doesn't necessarily have to be something particularly remarkable - as often as not memories will come flooding back. You'd be amazed by the level of detail that has stayed with people once they're reminded. I wouldn't ask David what happened. Instead I'd say: this happened. And then get him to recall the details: the emotions, the circumstances, what other people said and what he thought himself at the time. And, of course, it's always those details that bring a person's story and their personality to life on the page.

The only other ground rule was that David should trust me and commit to the project. He did and it was a very happy experience because he is the kind of bloke that whatever he does, he does properly. Having made the decision to tell his story, he told it properly and made sure we had the time we needed.

It is worth mentioning here that the mechanics of interviewing can vary from ghost to ghost. Some ghosts bring along a laptop and type while the interviewee speaks. Many other ghosts tape every meeting and then transcribe the interview later on. The tapers swear by this method as the best way to accurately get an author's voice. Leaving the recorder to do its work also means they can give their full attention to their subject and the questions they need to ask rather than focussing on details such as whether they have spelt 'deliberate' correctly.

Taping does, as one writer who is well known in the celebrity ghosting circuit admits, occasionally have its downsides. Machines are, after all, not infallible.

'I was recording a woman who had gone into great, tearful, detail about the sad break-up of her marriage. She was so upset and clearly still found every part of her story painful. I felt so sorry for her and was thinking all the way through, oh my god this is just awful. I should add, there was also a little voice inside me saying; the publishers are going to love this. It is just fantastic.

'The other bit of me was thinking, gosh this tape is going on for some time. When she had finished, I opened my tape recorder and the tape was broken. It hadn't recorded a thing. I had no choice. I had to ask her to do it all again. I didn't want to write it from memory because the subject had a certain way of talking and used particular phrases I knew I would never get quite right. God bless her, she did go through it all again. As it happened, the second take was actually better. She had got over the crying by then and thought it through a bit more clearly. Her recollections were more to the point.'

There is one other disadvantage to taping, beyond the purely technological. People can be quite intimidated by a little box on the table in front of them, recording their every word. Even well known authors, who may have been interviewed dozens of times before, will automatically become more guarded. Generally, over time, they will relax and perhaps even forget about the presence of the recorder. It is also possible for a ghost to speed up this process by assuring their author that the tape won't be played to anyone else and they do, of course, have final veto on any words used in the book.

Other ghosts, such as Lynne Barrett-Lee, don't use a laptop or a tape recorder. They find the technology a time consuming distraction.

I did tape one entire face-to-face interview on my phone once. When I played it back it was just two people rabbiting on, me almost as much as him and the only real nuggets were the ones I'd noted down anyway. Since then, I only ever tape meetings as a back up although I have had clients who like everything taped and wonder why I don't do the same. It's another diplomatic minefield, because everyone loves the sound of their own voice, but since I take copious notes and will rarely quote verbatim anyway, to me, it's an unnecessary intrusion. I am not conducting an interview to write a feature for a paper that requires verbal quotes; I'm going to 'inhabit' the subject. A very different thing.

I tend to pick out the salient points and then write the anecdote in a way that makes it sound more arresting on the page. People think they want you to capture the real them and I think I do, but I capture their voice as written, rather than as spoken. You don't write as you speak.

When I am interviewing I am completely focussed on 'gem-hunting', even though the collaborator might not see that. I remember, and highlight, all the bits where they say something interesting, and I think: that's definitely going in. Such treasures form the narrative skeleton which I can then begin to flesh out.

One piece of equipment no ghost can do without is a notebook and pen. This way, they can note down questions as they occur to them, while the author is talking and won't have to worry about forgetting them later on. All interviews head off down new avenues all the time, particularly in these early stages, so it is useful to keep a note of the good parts without interrupting an author who is in full flow. At a suitable break, the ghost can then return to the parts of the interview that caught his or her attention.

The length of interviews can vary, although initial ones are generally longer because there is a lot of ground to cover. Some authors are content to talk animatedly about themselves for hours on end. Others though are a spent force within just an hour or two. Any material gathered after that will be of noticeably poorer quality than at the start. The initial interview is the time for a ghost to get to know their subject fast and settle upon the optimum length for future ones. After a couple of hours it is quite easy to judge whether the subject has more left to give, or whether it is best to give it a rest and return to it at a better time. Sometimes, as ghostwriter Deborah Crewe relates, it may mean being quite forceful with reluctant speakers.

I have had people who get bored with talking about themselves. They get to the middle of an interview and say can we stop now? I tend to be a bit of a dragon and say no, we must keep going. Some people can only speak for short bursts though. It starts well, but they flag towards the end. Recalling a life can be a very intense thing.

From a ghosting point of view, you have all your questions prepared but even if they are all written down you do have to be ready to react to what the author says. You have to be alert to the moment you suddenly sniff a great story you had previously known nothing about and then pursue it. It can be quite tiring because you have to be constantly on the ball if you want to do a good job.

Collaborators need to think carefully about the location for this initial interview, not least because it may well set the scene for future ones. As discussed previously, ghosts like to immerse themselves in their author's life as part of the getting-to-know them process, so interviewing them in their own home is ideal. Aside from anything else, people are almost always more relaxed in familiar surroundings. Authors are often quite nervous in these early days, because they will be relating possibly intimate detail of their life to someone they don't yet know that well and will be eager to make a good impression on the ghost so the book has the best possible chance. Anything that puts them at ease is good.

Sometimes it is just not possible to meet at an author's house for a range of reasons ranging from the author not wanting others to know they are writing a book, to feeling it is too noisy or distracting there. In this case, the collaborators might like to meet in a neutral location such as a hotel lounge or coffee bar. Alternatively, if the author is well known and concerned about being recognised, or their private conversation being eavesdropped upon, a private room can be arranged within a hotel. On some occasions, ghosts will agree to install themselves for a weekend in a hotel local to the author so he or she can visit and talk for as many hours that are needed at their convenience. This concentrated form of interviewing isn't to everyone's taste, but can work well, particularly if an author's schedule is particularly tight. At the other extreme, if an author is wealthy and well connected, they may even invite their ghost to spend some time with them at their private residence in some far flung corner of the world. Ghosts describe finding themselves in the most surreal of settings, in millionaire playgrounds from Monaco to Bermuda. One ghost who worked on a wealthy businessman's biography found herself spending a week in Mauritius with her entire family.

'The author was always super busy doing one deal or another and the only time he could devote to his book was a couple of days in between meetings which he wanted to spend in Mauritius. I did already have a family holiday booked for that time, albeit in a far less glamorous location and he asked if I would consider switching it to Mauritius, with all our expenses paid. I wasn't about to say no. He put us up in an amazing hotel with a private speedboat at our disposal. I interviewed him for a few hours each morning and spent the rest of the time relaxing with my family in luxury. I did have to warn my kids not to get used to the lifestyle.'

In this first interview, one of the key points collaborators need to agree upon is the market for the book. Who will the reader be? A book is after all a commercial product and if neither the ghost nor author fully understands who the reader might be and what they like, the project will most likely head off in the wrong direction from the start. The ghost may well instigate a discussion around what other big names there are in this particular market and which of their books did particularly well, having done their own research prior to the interview. It is very useful to know more about the type of people a particular genre of books appeal to and why. It is also always illuminating for a ghost to hear which other books and authors their co-writer rates and why, too.

The other elements the ghost will look for in the first interview are the characters that will touch the main story (other than the main author) and how significant their role will be. There also needs to be a discussion around major themes, dates and settings. All of this information is essential to construct a chapter-by-chapter plan.

One of the toughest aspects to any book plan is working out where to begin and it is at this point that a ghost looks for a good idea of the most appropriate start point. Some life stories work best if told in chronological order but, even in non-fiction, the author is by no means tied to relating events as they happened. Other stories lend themselves to beginning with a significant event that will immediately grip the reader's attention and draw them into the narrative. The book can then use devices such as flashbacks to relate earlier events leading up to the dramatic opening.

Alternatively, if a book doesn't have an obvious narrative, it might be because it involves an argument. *Common Sense Rules* by Deborah Meaden is like many business books in that it isn't a straight biography, but rather an examination of a particular subject. In this case the subject in question is what it takes to run a successful entrepreneurial venture. The author, a star of TV's Dragons' Den, takes the reader through a range of elements that might contribute to the successful running of a company. *Common Sense Rules* doesn't have a beginning, middle and end, but is broken down into subject areas such as what makes a good business idea, building a team and getting investment, with each area taking up one chapter. In instances like this, the argument takes the part of the story. Running a successful business is the structural element that holds the book together.

Generally, non-fiction tends to be more loosely structured than its fictional cousin, the novel. Indeed, it may be the case that not every chapter will move the story or argument forward significantly, but it might be worth including. This is not a cue to neglect structure altogether though.

Authors shouldn't expect the chapter-by-chapter plan produced by their ghost after the initial interview to read like the blurb on the back of a book. It is not the *big sell* for their novel. It is a plan and should explain everything important that will go into each chapter in as few words as possible. It might even seem horribly bare, clinical even. That's fine. It's not trying to sell anything to anyone. It is just there to focus everyone's minds on structure and main content.

It is at this stage, on seeing the plan, authors sometimes question their ghosts and ask why they didn't include something from their views on subjects as diverse as feeding the poor and the spread of bovine TB. A ghost will have to gently remind them that while the half an hour diversion into these subjects was an interesting part of the initial interview, the views don't really have any place in a memoir about, say, the glamorous ups and downs in the music business. It is not uncommon for a new author to mistakenly believe that if a reader is interested in their story, they will probably be dying to hear their views on absolutely everything even if it is wholly unconnected to the day job. They won't. Apart from anything else, if the poor ghost is forced to shoehorn everything into the book it won't have a clean and clear direction. It will be a mixed and messy bag of disjointed jokes, anecdotes, observations and opinions. At the risk of labouring the point, that is why a plan is essential.

At the other end of the scale is an author who doesn't have very much to say on anything at all and this is the stage where ghostly alarm bells begin to ring. Ghost writer Neil Simpson says people who are dismissive, or downright disinterested in specifics are the most difficult to work with.

Writing a plan, or indeed a whole book, with someone who doesn't have much to say or who won't go into details is very difficult. They'll say, oh it happened sometime early in the Nineties and I'll say, I need to know exactly, but they refuse to be pinned down.

If this happens at the first interview, this is the stage when you can't help questioning whether their heart is in it, or they are just in it for the money because they got signed-up after their fifteen minutes of fame. You have to begin thinking about making a judgement call about how much you can realistically make up if they really won't give you very much. Sometimes you have to let your imagination take flight because that is all you have.

Another element that needs to be nailed down is the main characters in the book. The detail is not something to be included in the plan, but it is certainly something that needs to be thought about early on and raised in the interview. Authors, and well known ones in particular, might not understand why they need to attend to this. After all, they themselves are the star and their character will inevitably emerge through the narrative. However, as the beginning of this chapter emphasised, the reader doesn't truly know the author and, to be fair, neither does the ghost at this stage.

A ghost needs to know what gives the lead character their edge because, as with the main character in any novel, the reader has to believe they know what makes them tick. This is the moment for the ghost to ascertain what drives this person and what scares them. Are they a decisive person who plans everything down to the last detail, or do they tend to just fall into things? Are they by nature an optimist, or is their glass usually half empty?

A ghost will begin by delving gently into an author's background to discover what beliefs shape their lives and how were they forged. They will explore their upbringing, politics and prejudices. If the ghost can tease out any quirky details, so much the better. One ghost tells of interviewing a big name tycoon, who is worth billions of pounds, who was terrified, absolutely terrified, of calling room service when he stayed in a hotel. His poor wife had to regularly accompany him on his numerous business trips around the globe and would order-up room service while he locked himself in the bathroom in a complete panic.

'It wasn't a detail that went into his biography, but it told me more about the man than an hour discussing the various merits of certain accounting models,' the ghost said.

There is also a need to plot out the other characters who have a role in the book. The rule is, the more of a part they play in the main story, the more a ghost needs to know them. If someone only has a bit part, they decline in importance markedly and don't need an excessive amount of analysis.

It is helpful if the author paints a picture of his or her view of the people around them. It's not enough to say something along the lines of; yeah, well, my business manger is in his early forties, has dark hair, a bit of a stoop and can be quite feisty. If this person has an important part to play, the ghost needs to know more about his character and motivations. What makes this person tick, winds him up, or cools him down? How does he react under pressure? What is his backstory? The ghost also needs to know how the relationship between the pair developed, whether it ran smoothly, or if it was one battle of wills after another.

In any book, characters build up over time, layer by layer as the reader is invited to get to know them and understand their motivations. In a collaboration, a ghost needs to know if not the full details, at least the main points, from the beginning. They don't have the luxury of time to discover quirks and negative traits along the way. As far as possible, the author needs to give them full disclosure in the initial interview.

Right now is also the time to discuss how far the narrative can be stretched while keeping within the bounds of realism. In fiction writing it is common to ramp up the tension by adding new elements to the story, or an unexpected twist. The author of a work of non-fiction may not necessarily have a huge stock of arresting elements to grab the reader every chapter. Clearly they can't drastically alter the facts to improve the story, but there are things that can be done.

For a start, there should be a conversation between the collaborators about which points could be emphasised and maybe even exaggerated a little. There is obviously a line that can't be crossed here. It is not possible to completely alter or invent facts, but a certain amount of additional 'colour' can make all the difference. This is also the opportunity for collaborators to discuss which parts of the story might be best left out because they slow down the dialogue. Say the author spent twelve years scraping a living by singing in local clubs, before becoming an 'over night' sensation on X-Factor. The book should almost certainly concentrate the majority of its time on the TV show and its aftermath, rather than a tedious blow-by-blow account of endless evenings spent in Scunthorpe, Scarborough and Skegness. Although real life is lived in real time, minute by minute, a book can rush through the dull bits to get to the real meat of a story.

If there is any background material in existence, now is the time to hand it over to the ghost. It may come in the form of photos, documents, old emails or letters. Opinion is divided among ghosts as to whether they like to see any first drafts the author might have written in a stab at writing the book themselves, before deciding they needed professional help. Some find it an unwelcome distraction, while others find it gives them a useful direction in their questioning.

Occasionally, authors will have nothing on record at all. In this case a ghost will have to start the interview process from scratch and coax the story out bit by bit. It is up to a ghost to immediately pick up on any interesting angle an author might mention in passing. They can then focus their questioning on that episode and start to build a picture of the elements of the story they believe may interest the reader.

Although much of the information required for any book might be on tap, inside the author's head and will be gained through interviews, additional research is usually required. How much, or how little, depends a lot on the author and the subject matter. However, even if the author is very forthcoming, ghosts do usually find that doing a little research of their own does pay dividends, even if it only gives them help in the direction of their questioning. This was certainly the case when Caro Handley worked with Cynthia Lennon on her book *John*.

Cynthia Lennon was just about the only person who hadn't written a book about John Lennon even though she was married to the guy. Hodder & Stoughton wanted the definitive book about her life with John. I went out to Majorca to spend a week with her at her home there. We had a delightful time, sitting on her balcony sipping gin and tonics, but 40 years on she struggled to remember the kind of detail we needed to fill a long book. By the end of the week I was tearing my hair out.

When I got home I read every single book that I could that addressed that period in their lives. I read about John Lennon, the Beatles and everything that was going on around them at the time from the political situation to social developments. I went back and spent another week in Majorca and literally just fed questions and detail into her. I would say: I believe so and so happened on this day. She'd reply: oh yes, yes it did. Then I would probe her for her memories for how it felt to be at a particular event.

I needed to be able to ask questions like; what was it like the first time you made love with John Lennon. But to be able to ask something so intimate I needed to encourage her to recall the start of their romance, their friendships, family lives and their time at art college together. The technique is working the way into the detail by painting the bigger picture. You

have to refine it and refine it a bit more. It is the only way to work with someone who hasn't got a memory for detail.

This early planning and interview stage is among the most important parts of the whole ghosting process. It ensures the structure of the book is agreed from the start and both parties know what is expected from them. It's the ghost's opportunity to steer their author onto the right track and work with them to uncover the story everyone wants to hear. As ghost Nadene Ghouri explains, without this foundation, there is a real danger the whole project will go awry.

The worst thing that could happen to any ghost would be for a book to be published and then two months later the author to say 'I am not really comfortable with that, those are not really my words.' That would be a huge failure for a ghost. That is why you have to coach people carefully through the process.

Writing a book is a lengthy process, which can take many months. A well-written plan will act like a road map, guiding the ghost and the author on their journey together so they produce a well structured, full bodied, entertaining book.

Chapter Eight
Interviewing
Practicalities

A plan is, of course, just a plan until it is put into action. What comes next is an intensive interviewing process to get all the relevant detail out into the open, so a ghost can start to think how they will tackle their first draft. In an ideal world, the author would follow the previously agreed plan to the letter and obligingly talk through their life while sticking meticulously to the main points of the plan. This rarely, if ever, happens and it's up to the ghost to keep things on track over a series of interviews to tease out the necessary facts.

Very often ghosts find their co-authors don't immediately settle into the interview process. Even though a lot of the information required is on tap in the author's head, it takes time for the relationship to develop and the interviewee to relax. It is not unusual for authors to be extremely nervous and as a protective mechanism they may well retreat into anecdotes in these early stages. While anecdotes are always a pleasure and can light up a book, ghosts need to quickly steer the author towards more substantial detail. If a ghost doesn't take control at this stage, they are liable to end up with a tape recorder or notebook filled with a light-hearted stream of jokes which is almost impossible to weave into any sort of meaningful narrative. At the other end of the scale is an author who enters the process feeling it is vital to describe every day of his or her life in excruciating detail.

It is a challenge for any ghost to keep the interview process on track as Pippa, a ghost specialising in celebrity biographies, explains.

'Some people are natural anecdotists, which is great because that is what every ghost wants, lots of fantastic descriptive stories. However, you've got to be careful you don't end up with a whole bunch of fantastic one-liners. They are virtually impossible to weave together when you get to the writing stage. There are so many different storylines you'd drive yourself insane before you made any sense of them.

'Other authors are massively into detail and it is almost too much. I worked with a hugely successful athlete who remembered every single race she had ever run in, in incredible detail. It was amazing. It was all just there in her head. I guess athletes know their times and everyone else's times because they are so rigorously focussed over the years. It did make it quite difficult to focus on the main story though.

'The most difficult subjects though are the ones who give you virtually nothing. They'll say something like: I went to see the band. I'll say; what was it like? Was the room dark, smoky, or did it smell of pee? They'll shrug and say: well, you know what it is like. I know then I will have my work cut out. Extracting anything out of an author like this is going to be very difficult.'

The interview process can be challenging, intense and emotionally taxing for all sides. Ghosts need to invest a lot of time in research and preparation, so they are fully armed with the range of questions they want to ask ahead of each interview. However, flexibility will still be required, because hidden, and sometimes surprising, gems always emerge in interviewing, occasionally quite far down the line after the author and ghost have been talking together for weeks.

This is something I experienced after struggling for some weeks with how to portray the motivations of a woman who worked as an exotic dancer. After moving to the UK to escape a poverty-stricken upbringing in Brazil, the author, Cintia da Silva, made a large amount of money stripping for a range of wealthy clients and ended up working in some of the most glamorous spots in the world. Although Cintia's tale had many compelling elements from tragedy to triumph, plus strong female friendships and a glamorous, jet-setting lifestyle few people ever experience, it was initially difficult to get a book deal for her no holds barred biography *Full Brazilian*. Indeed, publishers who loved her rags-to-riches story said they struggled to find a sympathetic side to her character and worried a book about her life might not engage readers. In a bid to understand her better, I immersed myself into Cintia's life and work. I spent many hours with her in order to try to delve into what really made her tick, including spending evenings with her and her wealthy patrons at leading strip bars. It was only after a number of interviews that the full story emerged.

Once Cintia felt we had spent sufficient time together and finally fully trusted me, she started to talk about the tragic death of her two younger twin brothers when she was just 13-years old. They died in a terrible house fire and she blamed herself for their deaths because she had been unable to help them. More significantly, her family laid some of the blame at her door too, even though it seemed clear it was a terrible accident. It haunted Cintia her whole life. She never felt good enough for anything or anyone and for a long time was filled with self-loathing. Her insecurities coloured every choice and decision she made in her adult life. Just knowing something like this changed everything about the whole book in an instant.

Of course, building a relationship like this, can take time. Learning to trust and understand someone can take weeks and even years, although, with publishing deadlines racing towards an author, this process may have to be accelerated.

The total amount of time that ghostwriters need to spend interviewing their subjects varies from book to book and from author to author. Some collaborators prefer complete immersion and may spend weeks at a time locked away with the author. Other ghosts say that eight hours of solid talking will garner more than enough material for an 80,000-word book, as long as the interviews stay on topic and are utterly focussed. Occasionally, ghosts even move in with their subjects in an attempt to get them to knuckle down and tell their story. Clare, a magazine features journalist who ghosted the biography of one of the UK's well-known and best-loved actresses, had to do just that to get her subject to knuckle down and complete her book which had a high six figure advance.

'To begin with, the author insisted that she would write her own book, however because she was a well-known procrastinator, her agent brought in a beauty parade of ghosts. We got on very well, so I was chosen for what I was told was a 'long interview' to help her focus on the main parts of the story. I interviewed her and produced a lengthy document according to how I thought it would be structured. Then I heard nothing.

'Three months before the deadline for the book, she called me out of the blue. 'I suppose you had better write the whole thing,' were almost her first words to me. It was the beginning of a frantic process.

'One of the big problems was she was a fantastic performer, but she was a terrible interviewee. She treated me as though I was a member of her audience and rattled through one funny anecdote after the other. She didn't pause long enough to give me any detail though. I had to do what I did for magazine interviews and fill in the rest by talking to family and friends.

'Using what she told me, I wrote a version of the book as I thought it should be, but when I sent her a chapter, she would re-write it and send it back to me. I'd then claim it back from her and she'd claim it right back. In the end she said; 'we are never going to finish this thing unless you move in with me and stand over me'. I put my own life on hold and spent a week living in her house. It was crazy. I was fielding frantic emails from publishers and agents with one hand and reaching out to take a wine bottle out of her hands and pop it back into the fridge with the other.'

In plotting their line of questioning, there are a number of strategies open to ghosts. The first, and most obvious, is to work through their chapter-by-chapter plan, as outlined in the previous chapter. The ghost will alert the author that they will be, say, discussing chapters one, two and three at the next interview, so both sides have time to think about what needs to be said, according to the previously agreed structure.

An alternative strategy is for the author to talk through their life chronologically, from early childhood to the present day, regardless of the agreed structure. They might use one interview to discuss childhood and growing up, another to discuss early career and so on. Ghosts who favour this method say it is easier down the line when they are trying to locate material on tape, or in their notes. This chronological method is also useful when trying to find out more about an author's motivations. Say an author left school with virtually no qualifications, yet rose to become a millionaire captain of industry, it is really useful to tackle those childhood years early on to pin down what impact they had on that person's character. While the early years may be a small snapshot when the book is eventually written, there will be some essential detail here that needs to be teased out to shape what comes later. Similarly, if they had a bad relationship with their parents, or were abused or written off as a youngster, it will provide many clues to their later life.

There are, as ghost Caro Handley explains, times when a chronological approach just isn't appropriate.

Sometimes people are really thrown by a ghost saying; OK let's start with your childhood. They will say; no I don't want to talk about it. This is particularly the case with deeply personal stories where you have to go back to things that are often very tricky. I will often start with things the author likes to talk about. I'll say: tell me about that awards ceremony. My goodness, you looked amazing in that dress. You know you probably don't need all of what they'll say here, but it builds up a picture and begins a process of helping them feel more natural and relaxed. By the third session I will be able to ask; so what was

your dad like? By that time they will be more in the flow, more used to talking and get the idea.

There will always be moments when you have to say; tell you what, let's come back to that. At times like this is always helpful to have something safe up you sleeve; I've been meaning to ask you about so and so.

If there is a really grim backstory it is all part of the careful process of eliciting it while respecting the author's feelings. This may be the first time they have talked about it fully. Sometimes I do meet it head on and say: look, we are going to need to talk about this, I don't suppose it is going to be easy for you, but it is a critical part of your story.

If it helps I remind gently them that they don't have to write the book, they have a choice and can stop at any time, but if they're going to do it, then the story needs to be told. And once the story is out, I find the person is often relieved, they feel a burden has been lifted.

Ghosts sometimes prepare for each interview session by imagining themselves sitting down to write the chapters under discussion. This strategy forces them to think through the range of detail they'll need to know so they can formulate an appropriate list of questions. Authors can help this process along too, as Neil Simpson found when he worked with a fireman.

We lived quite a long way from each other, so it wasn't always easy to meet. Before any meeting we

THE COMPLETE GUIDE TO GHOSTWRITING

did have the fireman would email me in advance with maybe 18 or 20 stories. It would be just one-liners, with headings like: 'flock of swans in OAP home', or 'cow in slurry pit'. When we did meet up, we would sit down and go through each one. I'd say: 'OK, number one, flock of swans in the home' and he'd say, 'oh yes, right..' and off he would go. He was great because he was very aware of what kind of book it was going to be and the stories he was telling. There was structure to the process too, which was really helpful.

Knowing how to craft the right questions to unlock the information from an author's mind should be at the core of a ghost writer's toolkit. Very often a subject won't know which parts of their story are relevant, or may even be reluctant to go into detail on certain parts of their life story. It's up to a ghostwriter to tease it out.

Occasionally, no matter how deeply a ghost delves, it just won't be possible to iron out all the inconsistencies in a story. In a case like this, the collaborators will have to take a view on what to include in the book and what to leave out. This was certainly something Tim Tate found when he was working with Sarah Forsyth for the book *Slave Girl* which was discussed in chapter five.

I interviewed a number of people to build a picture of Sarah's story. One of the things that didn't make any sense was that her mum Thelma said she had received phone calls from Sarah throughout the year that Sarah worked as a prostitute in Amsterdam.

Sarah has absolutely no memory of that and doesn't believe she would have been allowed by her captors to make phone calls. I spent a long time looking at it and thinking: how can I deal with this? The only honest way to deal with it is to put it exactly as that. It didn't make sense. Thelma said she had phone calls, but Sarah said she didn't make any phone calls and wasn't allowed to.

We will never know the truth of it. As a writer, you have to be honest, lift the skirts and show the working out. Sometimes, you have to say; this is life in the raw, it is messy but there doesn't seem to be an explanation for it. I didn't want it to undermine the credibility of what happened and at the same time I didn't want to ignore and hide it away because it didn't fit. Honesty is the best policy.

As well as knowing the value of preparing well before they get in front of a subject (i.e. not just hoping for the best the named author will tell all), effective interviewing is all to do with crafting questions that dig below the surface information, or the stories everyone already knows. A skilled ghostwriter needs to couch their questions in a way that the interviewee feels comfortable answering, while thinking ahead to supplementary questions by interpreting verbal and non-verbal clues along the way. Planning, preparation and anticipation are essential.

The best questions to gather information for a book are often open-ended. They begin with words like 'how?' 'what?' 'where?' and 'when?' as conversation starters that encourage expansive answers that produce an abundance of information. Again, if a ghost is experienced and has done their homework, they will have found out as much information as they can about the facts surrounding key events beforehand. It would be a waste of everyone's time if they had to ask the author for details about what is already in the public domain, or to keep stopping their flow to ask the nitty gritty of what happened next such as names, dates and detailed, yet already available, factual information. It's far better to say; 'this is what happened, how do you remember it exactly?' or 'how did you feel when you saw the newspaper headline exposing your affair?' It might seem blunt, reading it here in black and white, but authors are always grateful if their collaborator gets straight to the point.

The last thing a seasoned ghost will do is put an author on the spot with a close-ended question that kills an interview dead. For this, think about something along the lines of: Did you embezzle the company's money? That sort of questioning should be saved right to the end of the whole interview process and only if the subject has not yet explained the circumstances of their story fully. Frankly, though, if the ghost didn't get to the bottom of that sort potentially explosive element of an author's history earlier, the chances are the whole process has gone sour anyhow.

The worst questions, as every wise ghostwriter knows, are the double, or even triple-barrelled showstoppers. For example: 'Why did your security team use violence against your fans? Did you know that was going to happen? Did you give the order?' Clumsy questions like this give interviewees carte blanche to avoid the question they want to ignore and let's them choose the less difficult one. Not only does this signal the relationship between the ghost and the author isn't likely to progress very effectively, it doesn't bode well for the final product.

Meanwhile, having asked the question, ghostwriters should always know when to shut up and listen to the answer. This is another of those core journalistic skills that translate so effectively to ghosting. To get an idea of how effective this can be, it's worth watching the 1976 movie, '*All the Presidents Men*', which focuses on two Washington Post reporters investigating corruption in the Nixon government. There is a great moment when Bob Woodward (played by Robert Redford) is in the newsroom, on the phone to a Nixon fundraiser and he asks how his $25,000 cheque wound-up in the Watergate money trail. He is then silent and stays silent. It is a dangerous, not to mention agonising moment, that feels like it might go on forever. Then, the man on the other end of the phone finally blurts out the truth, even though it is highly incriminating.

Learning when to keep quiet does take some skill, not least because in the relationship-building process ghosts are always tempted to help their authors out by prompting them when they look stuck for an answer. Doing so will not always help get the best story though. This is not to suggest ghostwriters 'trick' their subjects into telling their story either. It is merely that sometimes, particularly with awkward memories, it pays to give people time to talk. They'll probably even welcome the technique. People hate silences and will rush to fill them, even if it means they have to take a deep breath and say something they never thought they'd say out loud. It's an old journalistic technique, but silence really does open many doors.

Something that can and does frequently happen, often to an author's complete surprise and embarrassment, is they suddenly dissolve into tears. They'll be happily talking about their favourite childhood teacher one moment and the next second they will be sobbing uncontrollably, crying in a way they may not have done for years. It happens much more often than anyone would expect.

Talking extensively about events that have shaped their lives can have a powerful affect on any author, however well they may feel they have compartmentalised or rationalised them. Very often, they will not have vocalised these moments for years, if ever, and it can prove a painful experience to articulate them after a long period. Reliving these old memories can lead to a sudden release of raw emotion and it is for this reason that it is not uncommon for an author to be reduced to tears at some point during the interview process and possibly several times.

Although any outbursts or out-pouring of emotion might feel awkward and embarrassing for the author, particularly the first time it happens, it shouldn't faze a ghost one bit. Indeed, most experienced ghosts will have seen this sort of reaction many times before while conducting interviews for their previous work. The most professional way for a ghost to deal with it is to let the emotion run its course, but continue the interview. In other words, they will keep the tape recorder running, or the notebook/laptop poised, because the author's reaction indicates the ghost has probably reached the nub of the interview. It may sound cynical, but this is the bit the reader wants to know. When they buy a book they want to understand what touches and motivates the author and this is undoubtedly it. It is the ghost's task to gently probe into the background of the story, while remaining sensitive to the feelings of the author.

It is an absolute no no for the ghost to start blubbing, however upsetting the material presented to them. Indeed, as ghost Caro Handley says, she was spectacularly warned off from showing any sort of emotional reaction by one author.

Hodder and Stoughton brought me in to work on *Behind Closed Doors* with Jenny Tomlin, the mother of EastEnders actress Martine McCutcheon. It was a gritty story of Jenny's childhood in East End of London in the early Sixties where her father's violent beatings, humiliations and sexual abuse were the reality of daily life. I was the third ghost she had and

when the publisher first told me about the job they warned me she could be a bit of a tricky customer. They said she could be a real terrier and that was an understatement.

I went to her house to meet her and the moment I walked in she said; right, first things first, you are not going to cry are you? The last person cried and I don't need that. I said no, absolutely not, and from then on we got on very well, in fact Jenny turned out to be funny, interesting and to have great recall.

To be honest I wouldn't dream of crying when someone tells their story, however grim; the last thing an author should have to do is, feel awkward or comfort the ghost. The ghost has to remember that this is not about them or their feelings – if you need to cry, do it later.

Some authors may take time to warm up to their subject and may even be reticent to reveal the details of what has haunted them for years. It may take a few sessions to build up trust on both sides but, in a good ghosting relationship, once authors open up and begin to talk about themselves it is often the case they just can't stop. Indeed, they may very well welcome the opportunity to voice stories they may have kept hidden for years. If a ghost listens patiently and is sympathetic to their co-writer, they will undoubtedly earn the enduring respect and gratitude of the named author. The subject of the book will no doubt be supremely grateful to finally get everything off their chest in such a painless manner. Indeed, it is not unusual for a ghost to be told at the end of a project that writing in collaboration has been like a form of therapy. Indeed, as one author once told me: 'it is like therapy that gets published. Ego and psychology all helped out at once.'

It probably helps authors that they are speaking in the full knowledge that the person doing the listening is utterly non-judgemental and only interested in hearing what they have to say. Plus, not a single word can be exposed to the outside world without their say so. The author does, after all, have the right of approval on the final manuscript.

None of this is to say that, in some cases, a ghost won't find themselves deeply moved by the subject under discussion. Indeed, they frequently will. Any sort of extensive interviewing is an intense process, which requires a ghost to fully understand and empathise with an author's story and occasionally it can be overwhelming. Ghostwriter Shannon Kyle, for example, describes how she had to reconsider the projects she took on after being deeply affected by *Nobody Cared,* a real life memoir of a girl who had suffered a long period of sustained and harrowing abuse.

My background as a journalist means I have heard a lot over the years, so I thought I was pretty hardened to most things. However hearing first hand accounts of child abuse is never easy at times, especially when graphic details are involved. Another time an author told me she had told me more than her counsellor, which is both an honour and a position of responsibility as a ghost.

Katy Weitz who has ghosted a number of bestselling inspirational memoirs, including *Daddy's Little Secret* and *Mummy is a killer*, says she has come to terms with the sometimes difficult material by reminding herself that she is providing an invaluable service to an author by helping to give them a voice.

A lot of the time it is the voice they have always been denied. I use my skills as a storyteller to translate their emotions onto the page. When I feel I have done a good job, I get an enormous sense of satisfaction and well-being. Plus, they always get out in the end. When I am deep into the horror of it, I tell myself it will come right. Then, when they escape and achieve freedom, I feel the weight lifting off my own shoulders just a little.

Sometimes a ghost might have to halt an interview for a composure break. On face value, this might not seem ideal because it may break up the flow of an interview a little, but it is fine. In fact, it is a good sign the ghost fully understands the subject and has empathy with the author. The emotional reaction will help them in the writing process because they will be better equipped to get across the depth of feeling surrounding a story.

Authors who feel uncomfortable, or even under pressure, during an interview may like to remind themselves that the onus is not on them to dictate an entire book, or to recall dialogue word-for-word. A ghost is looking for the main bones of each of their stories and will use them to write a fuller picture. Any additional detail though is, of course, a bonus.

Ghosts have many tried and tested methods to capture material from even the most reluctant subject. As Katy Weitz discovered, sometimes it is as simple as switching off any recording devices and having a relaxed chat.

The time when you just come out of the interview is often the most productive. The machine will go off and the author will visibly relax. That's when things start to pop out. Sometimes, when they are in full flow I try to surreptitiously switch the recorder back on.

When I was working on *Cellar Girl* with Josefina Rivera the thought that I wasn't 'getting' something plagued me throughout the interview process, but I just didn't know what it was. It is the extraordinary story of a young mum-of-three who was held in a cellar along with five women and starved, beaten and repeatedly raped to fulfil her captor's desire of creating a large family. Girls were dying around her and it was a real horror show. She told the story with perfect frankness and great eloquence, but I knew something was missing. I couldn't figure out what I couldn't hear. On the last day of interviews I was desperately asking all sorts of random questions in a bid to get to the bottom of it.

By the time the tape was switched off I realised I was still missing something crucial to make the story whole. I needed something else to define it. We went out for lunch together and started talking, quite by chance, about New Years Eve. Suddenly, Josefina just came to life and started talking about how she

loved taking fairground rides with the family. Finally I could see it and hear it. This was the glimpse of her I had been waiting for. I grabbed my Dictaphone while she was talking and let it run.

What I was looking for all along was a sense of well-being to end it all. I had to bring the reader out of it and let them breathe again, otherwise it would just all be too dark and horrible. The fact that she is out of it and OK was the light I was missing.

A ghostwriter is, in many ways, like a ventriloquist in that they try to capture the character of their subject, if not their exact words. Indeed, very often, it is the ghost who adds the all-so-important bones to the meat of a story. They'll get the main points from their interviews with the author, but then, later on they'll add the detail. From a scant description of something like an escape in the dead of night they will add the important detail which will bring the story alive. What did it smell like in that bustling, Third World airport? What were the sounds that filled the air? How did the guards look as they eyed the fleeing family?

Oddly, it is often this, entirely made-up, detail that the authors like most when they review the finished article and many ghosts speak of how they've heard their own additions trotted out in media interviews, as though they were the author's own recollections.

As Flora, a ghost specialising in celebrity biographies explains, a ghost's imagination can be a powerful weapon.

'I had a Post It note stuck to my computer for ages, with a quote from another ghost I'd met. It said: if in doubt, make it up. I would probably say something less blunt like: elaborate, but you get the picture.

'It is surprising how much a ghost can effectively elaborate. There are events and emotions we all have in common, like our feelings on the first day at school, or starting a new job, or when a first child is born. Even if we haven't had direct experience of some things, we can often imagine what it was like.

'Even so, I was surprised when I heard an author I had worked with, talking on Desert Island Discs about something I had written. I had gone into detail about their feelings about a particular event in their life and I knew the bits they were relating had come entirely from my imagination, yet now they completely believed it was their own thoughts. It is quite a complement really.'

In a more extreme example of this, another ghost, David Long, recalls how, even after hours of interviews, one author he worked with completely 'forgot' his book was ghosted at all. The book had gone on to win a substantial prize too.

The book in question became a complete bible on a particular subject and I confess even I was surprised it had done so well. It was one of my first ghosted books and, although a lot of the information was from the client, an awful lot came from my research and input too.

The book won a very prestigious award in America. I admit it does grate a little whenever he talks to me now and calls it 'my book'. I say to him: I am the only person on the planet you can't say that to. Say it to your wife, or your publisher, or anyone else you want to, but you can't say that to me. When we talk, it is 'our book'.

I am not bothered about not having my name on the cover, or any public acknowledgement. I do honestly think he has literally forgotten he hadn't written it though.

Occasionally, authors may need help from other sources to jog their memories, or to add a layer of detail. Depending on the story, ghostwriters may also interview people who have a close connection with the author, such as friends and family. They might also visit a childhood home, or some key locations in the story, to experience them for themselves and help them build up the picture. In some cases, the culture or environment an author grows up in, or inhabits as an adult, may be quite different from anything a ghost has ever experienced before. If a ghost sees at least part of it first hand, it will help them plan interviews more effectively. There may be many things an author takes for granted, but may not realise they are unusual to other people. By immersing themselves into their territory, a ghost will spot this and raise it as an issue in the interviews. Similarly, if the ghost can see and experience some of the colour of a story for his or herself, they can then concentrate their interviewing energies on getting down into the detail of the author's own story rather than getting bogged down into locations, trends and sensual experiences.

Additional research does not replace the need for a coherent and interesting narrative and the best way to get this is via a thorough interview process. Authors shouldn't expect their ghosts to stuff in a load of superfluous detail on an area's history and cultural shifts to pad out the main story. It won't fit in and it will stand out a mile unless the book itself is a social history commentary. The best source of research for the story is always the author themselves and they need to put the time in.

By the end of the interview process, depending on the way the ghost records an author's recollections, there should be well in excess of 80,000 to 100,000 words of available material, consisting of stories, short anecdotes, dialogue and descriptions of key events and characters. There may even be an accompanying bundle of research, photos, letters and other aide memoires to assist the co-writer. The next task is to begin to sort this rich jumble of information into a readable, and hopefully highly enjoyable, format. It is time for the ghost to begin the first draft.

CHAPTER NINE
CHALLENGES OF TELLING
A STORY

Getting the structure right and the interviews in the bag are just the first hurdle in any ghosting collaboration. The next hurdle is the rather daunting prospect of turning the mass of disjointed information gleaned from the author into an interesting manuscript of 80,000 words or more. For this aspect of the job it is almost 100 per cent over to the ghost. This is the time when the author can kick back and relax for a short while.

Perhaps, hardly surprisingly, many ghosts say getting started on the writing can be one of the most difficult parts of their job as the enormity of the task stretches before them. Generally, though, once they have knuckled down and got at least the first half of the words drafted, things start to get a little easier. All being well, they get into the rhythm of the job and the words will flow as they shape the first draft.

'First draft' is an interesting phrase in itself and it is worth examining it a little more closely here. It implies the ghost goes away, re-jigs the interviews into some sort of coherent order and then sends their initial stab at the book back to the author to take a look ahead of a further discussion. Nothing could be further from the truth. When an author sees the first draft from their ghost, whether it is a single chapter, or the whole thing, it will most likely be the third, fourth, or even sixth draft of the section in question. Why? Well, because any manuscript presented to a client needs to be polished and as close to the finished product as possible. As any ghost will attest, showing a client a half-finished, or very rough, draft is the easiest way to get their authors running for the hills, or at the very least demanding extensive re-writes.

Opinion is mixed about how far into the writing process a ghost gets before they present an author with the work. Some ghosts, such as Douglas Wight, swear by the approach of sending over work on a chapter-by-chapter basis on the grounds that any potential problems will be picked up at the earliest opportunity.

I like to involve the author as much as possible. I write a chapter and send it to them so they can look at it while I am getting on with the next one. Sometimes I get people who file stuff back to me so quickly, I end up working on loads of bits at once. That can be challenging. I'll be dealing with complaints and corrections while trying to get on with the new stuff. There are authors who take a bit more time coming back or who are just happy to let you get on with it.

Those are the times when I think there may be something to be said for doing the entire project and then sending it in one go.

Others, such as Neil Simpson, prefer to complete the whole book first so the manuscript is in the best shape it can be as a whole. The thinking behind this is it is quite likely there will be some chopping and changing between chapters further down the line as a ghost gets to know the material better and adjusts the structure accordingly. It makes sense to hold back the manuscript until it can be reviewed in one go, with everything in its proper context. Of course, as Neil admits, having got this far, it is always a bit scary giving the author the first sight of a completed manuscript.

I always feel it is better to give the author the whole thing, although occasionally I might give them the opening chapter earlier on. Sending any copy over is horrific and terrifying though. You never know what they are going to think. It is their life and I have written it in different words.

I have saved three messages on my answering machine from clients who have called after they have first read their book. They were saying how much they loved it and it is always such a huge relief to hear that.

The half way house between these routines is for a ghost to provide an author with the first three chapters and the publisher too, if there is one on board, so all sides can make sure they are happy.

As one publisher said: 'if the first three are OK, the rest will flow. Everyone will trust each other and even if the book does run into a problem later on, it will probably be quite straight forward to sort it out. Once I know everyone is on board with the first three chapters, I don't need to see it again until it is finished.'

The process of producing a completed first draft of the entire book usually takes between three and six months, although ghosts can sometimes be called upon to turn a book around in a matter of a few weeks. This would be particularly true in the case where there is a celebrity that is currently in the headlines and publishers are keen to capitalise on public curiosity. In chapter five Shannon Kyle talked about how she had just three weeks to produce the first draft of Jade Goody's autobiography in the weeks leading up to the reality TV star's death. Neil Simpson turned around Christoper Biggins' biography *Just Biggins: My story* in just four weeks. The comedy actor's career was flying high with an unexpected revival after he became the 2007 winner of *I'm a Celebrity… Get me out of here!*

Writing a book this quickly is all down to the skill of the author. In other projects, I have had subjects who have been very difficult, who haven't got much to say, or don't speak very much at all. It is like getting blood out of a stone. It is impossible to turn a book around quickly in a case like that. Luckily, Biggins was an old pro right from the start. He never

missed a single appointment and was always ready to give his all.

He timed every appointment to the minute. If we had set aside two hours between 10 and 12 he would, in the nicest possible way, give me the two hours. He kicked off with the briefest possible 'hello, how are you' and then got straight into the action. He'd say: 'OK, where did we leave off. Oh yes, on the 28th of December that year I moved to London and got this curious flat….' Then, at 12 O'clock an alarm would go off and we would be all done for the day. It was brilliant and made it a lot easier that he had a lot to talk about. He was old school and had had a really good life.

I didn't have time to transcribe my notes and write them up. I just went back and wrote what I had before returning the following day for the next instalment.

Most people would imagine that the bulk of a ghost's time during the more usual three to six month writing window is taken up in writing the first draft of the manuscript, but this isn't the case. Generally, around half of the time is spent getting down the full story in the correct order and the rest of the time is spent in editing the copy.

Editing in this case is not a case of simply checking on grammar, doing a detailed spell check and cutting out a bit of excess verbiage. It can be a very involved process indeed. Every word, sentence and paragraph needs to be sense checked. Ghosts must test the behaviour, dialogue and reactions of characters are consistent and in tune what the reader might expect, particularly in the case of the main character, the author. If it is someone in the public eye, the reader will have firm views on what they expect their heroes to think, feel and say. Ghosts will also go through any key events featured to check them for pace and credibility.

If they haven't done so already, this is also the time for a ghost to check and re-check the facts of each story. Although ghosts are working in full collaboration with an author, they need to make certain stories aren't, well, the polite way of putting it would be: 'over-exaggerated'.

There will always be an element of exaggeration in any story telling and it is worth noting that, in most cases, these embellishments are not done in a malicious or deliberately misleading way. Every one of us has a tendency to conveniently forget some events, while talking-up others and most of the time it doesn't cause any offence. After all, who doesn't want to be seen as, say, funnier, more interesting or more attractive to the opposite sex? There are many other reasons why people alter their memories to suit the version of themselves they like. It may even be perfectly innocent because the actual facts have been clouded through the mists of time. Alternatively, someone may be a little insecure about their current position and will deliberately try to make their circumstances seem more important. When authors tell the odd white lie, it may simply be that they want to forget about all they went through on route to get where they are today; all the rubbish jobs, the piles of rejections and verbal knock backs.

Whatever the reasons for the exaggeration, truth is a big issue in ghostwriting. While ghosts have to empathise with their subjects and recognise they will undoubtedly want to seem more successful, or more interesting than they are, no one should allow themselves to be drawn into writing out-and-out fiction when it is being presented as fact. Embellishing a story is fine in a conversation between friends and souping up a story is OK as long as it doesn't go too far. However, when something is recorded in print and the facts are blatantly wrong it could well infringe libel laws and that is something neither the ghost or an author wants. We will look at the legal side of things in more depth in chapter 10, but for now it is worth touching on how both ghosts and authors should stick to the facts as far as humanly possible.

If there are any doubts about the circumstances around an event, a ghost should raise them immediately. Not in a hostile way, as an accusation, but by way of clarification. They might say: 'In the last interview you mentioned that you married your wife the day after you'd met in Las Vegas, but just now you mentioned you were childhood sweethearts in Plymouth. I just wanted to get that right, because if I get confused, the reader might too….' Ghosts should never be nervous about pointing out inconsistencies, because, apart from anything else, if they are unconvinced by the author's version of events, they've got no hope of unravelling it for the poor reader.

The absolute rule here is: if it is not possible for a ghostwriter to stand up the truth of a story, then they should leave it out. A good test of this is to imagine an anecdote being printed on the front page of tomorrow's newspapers. If that sounds like a recipe for a writ, then a ghost should leave the offending material on the cutting room floor. As a ghost, you have to get that right, or you'll be out of a job. It's a hard line to walk, but it is the right one.

This is not to say that occasional slight exaggerations can't be left to ride. As Andrew Crofts says, they can often be vital for a good narrative.

You have to accept that everybody adjusts their stories to a certain extent. If you wrote what they said exactly as it happened, blow-by-blow, it would produce the most tedious book on earth.

Luckily, most of the time, it is quite easy for a ghost to spot when an amazing story doesn't quite add up. James, a ghost who specialises in memoirs of sports stars, relates how one former footballer told him the same story every week. He knew pretty much straight away that something was not right, because each time the anecdote featured a completely different character. One week the hero of the tale was Bobby Charlton, then George Best and then Wayne Rooney. In a case like this, it is best to do as James did and tactfully leave the story out.

If there are question marks over a number of facts, a ghost may well return to the author to check them. This may occur at various points during the writing period, before they show them the first draft. This is a perfectly acceptable, normal part of the process and very often small queries can be cleared up by an exchange of emails, or via brief telephone conversation. At this mid way stage there may well be other gaps to fill in too. Perhaps, for example, the author may have mentioned something during the interviews which a ghost hoped to return to at a later point and then failed to do so after getting distracted by another story. If a ghost is in touch to check a handful of queries, it is a good opportunity to go back and highlight the topic that previously dropped off the radar. Similarly, now the writing has begun and the ghost has more idea of how the book is flowing, they may decide they need more detail on a particular incident. That aspect of the story may not have seemed significant earlier, but further down the line it may gain significance and appear to have a greater bearing on the overall narrative.

The defining moment for any ghost is when they send the first draft to the author. After weeks, or months, of being the only person to have read the manuscript, it can be utterly nerve wracking to let another person see it, particularly when the first reader will be the person who is likely to be the most critical. And, any material must go to the named author first, before it goes anywhere else. It is, after all, their book and they have the right to see it before anyone else.

Even experienced ghosts admit they get nervous when they click the 'send' button and the manuscript goes to the author. They will be filled with self-doubt. What if they hate it? Or, once they see it on the page, will they get cold feet over their revelations? However, ghost Caro Handley says this is the point where subsuming one's ego is most important.

People often say that ghostwriting is a profession where you can't afford to have ego and this is the time where this is most important. It is not the ghost's book. They don't have the by-line. They can't send over the draft thinking; this is really good, I will be furious if they don't like it.

I say to people I write for, this is all still open at this stage. Don't panic if you feel it isn't what you want it to be, or there is something you really don't like. This is where we talk about it and you tell me what you think.

It does happen. Everything will seem fine while the ghost and author are talking it all through in the security of a home, or office, but once the story get put on the printed page, some authors have been known to freeze in terror. The enormity of what they are about to reveal of themselves hits them and occasionally authors can begin backtracking in a major way. In the worst-case scenario, it can even lead to a complete breakdown in the relationship between author and ghost, meaning the project is aborted at the 11th hour.

Nearly every ghost has had experience of author jitters and it can be deeply uncomfortable for both parties. To make matters worse, authors are sometimes unwilling or unable to articulate what it is that is really bothering them about the book. They may just have an uneasy feeling about it because the intense scrutiny of their life simply makes them feel even more vulnerable, yet not know how to explain what it is that bothers them. In this case, they may well resort to nit-picking over largely irrelevant detail which will quickly erode their relationship with their co-writer. Others will know exactly what it is that bothers them and will have no qualms about criticising a ghost for the way they have charted significant events in their life. Seeing it on the printed page is just too raw.

Nancy, who ghosted a true life story about the exploits of a female high flyer, found her relationship with the author deteriorated rapidly once she filed the first draft.

'To begin with everything was perfect and we got on really well. On the day we were first introduced, we went for a drink after the meeting and she took my arm as we walked down the street, chatting away like we were old friends.

'I sent her the first draft and she changed completely. She wanted to make changes on every other sentence. She was saying: 'I don't wear Ray Bans, I only ever wear Dior sunglasses.' Or: 'There are no corner baths in any New York hotel room.' I could have been there for another month and I would never be able to make all the changes she wanted. I kept saying; it is your book and we need to make it the way you want. We are a team, let's work together. She wasn't interested though. I suspect she saw the story in black and white and decided it was too racy, but I only wrote what she told me.'

Well known authors in particular can get cold feet at this stage, as they worry how certain, less palatable parts of their character might play out in the public domain. Caro Handley faced just this situation in a book she collaborated on with a celebrity author.

There are always the bits they want to tell you and the bits they don't. He had deliberately not said anything about a daughter by his first marriage who he had effectively abandoned. He only wanted to mention her in passing, but I had to sit him down and say, people will actually think better of you if you address it. This is what you need to say.

I suggested he was very open and said he had really screwed up and really wished he'd had a relationship with her. It took a bit of persuading to get it in the book, but he did it in the end. He just needed his hand holding through the process of what to say and how to say it.

Interestingly, a few of the reviews said how touching it was that he had acknowledged his feelings about abandoning his daughter. If an author is willing to show vulnerability, the reader thinks better of them.

If he hadn't done this, I think readers would have realised his daughter was left out and felt cheated.

Occasionally, an author will just not like the book that has been written and won't want to continue because they can't see a way to resolve it with the ghost writer. This is clearly a terrible outcome for both sides, but unfortunately, as in any creative process, there are never any guarantees every project will turn out perfectly. There are always one or two that don't work out as anyone would have hoped. It does, however, happen very infrequently.

If a project does break down, the author and ghost will have to make a financial agreement that will satisfy both sides and this may have to be brokered via an agent if relations are particularly strained and there is more information on the legal implications of this in the next chapter. Once both parties go their separate ways, the author will have to decide if they want to go through the whole process again, or abandon their ambitions altogether, while the ghost will have to pick themselves up and go on to the next project.

Publishers are sympathetic to authors when they get cold feet. Indeed, according to HarperCollins publisher Natalie Jerome, it is not an unusual experience for any writer, ghosted or otherwise.

It can be an emotionally laborious process for everyone involved: author, ghost and publisher too. Most of the time, the author will feel confident and happy at every stage right up until when the book hits the shelves. Sometimes though, you do get a situation

where they are not happy. They may not feel the ghost has captured their voice. Or, it could be they have and it is just the experience of seeing it in writing that they find quite hard.

It is not scientific. I could look at a couple of chapters of someone's book and it will seem to read perfectly well in my opinion, but the author will completely disagree. Often it is a case of sifting through the anxiety around the actual process, which I am very sympathetic with, to determine the hard cold facts of whether the book is any good from a literary perspective.

Something both ghosts and publishers are agreed on is the best way to see off any potential shocks at this stage is to make it very clear right from the start what publishing a life story really means. Lynne Barrett-Lee says she always sits her authors down at the start of the collaborative process to give them what she calls a 'no holds barred talk'.

It is a hard-hitting meeting because once we've both invested time in the project I don't want to get to a situation where they see the work and start backtracking and taking all the meat out of the book. I say; this is what you are doing, your family will be reading it, your friends will be reading it and your enemies will be reading it. There is no point trying to use the book as a platform to get back at people you hate either as there will be fall-out you might not be prepared for.

I sort out all those things at the beginning to avoid problems later on. I am also very clear on how I work and what my role is. I am their most avid reader, to some extent, asking the questions a reader would, diplomatically steering the narrative so that it sings on the page; it's hard to be objective about what is and isn't fascinating about your own life. I'm sure I'd be no different! Creative control is therefore an important thing to establish early on. If the subject finds that hard to swallow then they are probably better off finding a different ghost.

Publishers also adopt a similar approach to head off any later wobbles from an author.

Preface publisher Trevor Dolby describes how he and his team puts in a series of back-ups to ensure there are no surprises when the author first gets sight of any initial material. He calls it a game-plan and its entire focus is on helping an author understand the realities of putting their life story in print.

At the outset, any first time author feels the thrill of being published. They like the idea that they are going to tell their story and be paid for it. Right then though, there are just a handful of people involved. They'll be excited about working with them and about the process. Then, suddenly, they think, oh my goodness this is going to be seen by a lot of people and it is not just this cosy thing just between the few of us. As a publisher, you have to cater for that.

We spend a lot of time talking about what points we think this is going to happen and how will it happen. This is not a conversation that we hold with the author particularly. That would be rather crass. We talk about it among ourselves and we try to put in a strategy for getting around these things. The books I've been involved with have never ground to a halt thanks to planning and personality. You have to be terribly assiduous.

On the odd occasions where misunderstandings or disputes arise between a ghost and the author, the publisher or agent may have to intervene. This can occur when a ghost believes strongly that one particular story should be included, but an author gets cold feet. Obviously the final say lies with the author, but it is quite possible the ghost will attempt to present some persuasive arguments in favour of a particular thread. If the publisher or agent can be similarly persuaded the material will help the saleability of the book, they may also weigh in to persuade a reluctant author. Alternatively, they may well come up with a compromise which will appease both parties.

It is very rare for a project to be abandoned altogether because a ghost and author can't see eye to eye and even more so at this late stage when there is a completed manuscript at stake. Generally, if there is any mismatch, it should become obvious very early on and the two parties can go their separate ways with no harm done.

All being well, things won't ever get that bad between a ghost and author and the worst that will happen is the author will want to make a few minor changes to the copy. According to ghost writers, the course of events here usually follows a similar pattern. The author will tell a ghost they want to make 'a number of changes' and the ghost might well feel a rising sense of panic wondering how extensive the edit will be. Quite aside of how it might impact the carefully crafted manuscript, there is also the question of the publishing deadline. When deadlines are tight, there is no time for extended sessions between the author and ghost going backwards and forwards to hone the copy to perfection. So, while a ghost takes a deep breath and awaits the changes with trepidation, the author will begin to go through the manuscript page by page, either manually, or via the electronic version. Then, to the ghost's relief, it frequently turns out that the 'number of changes' are perhaps just one or two minor edits on each page that are actually quite easy for them to deal with. It may take just a few hours to incorporate them into the main copy.

This pattern of events is usually down to the author's natural and understandable desire to stamp their mark on the book that bears their name. By taking control of at least part of the writing process, they inevitably feel closer to the end product and more confident about taking ownership. Some ghosts pre-empt this need for author involvement by leaving questions in the margin via the track changes or comment functions, so the author can answer short queries on the copy. Again, it is all part of helping an author feel part of the writing process.

Of course, at the other end of the scale in the story of the submission of the first draft and edit, is the fact the author has to read their book in the first place. Former US President Ronald Reagan, when asked about his (ghosted) memoir famously said; 'I hear it's a terrific book. One of these days I'm going to read it myself.'

Although authors entrust ghosts with their life story, there are occasional incidences where celebrities have freely admitted they haven't actually read the book that bears their name and these authors have to be told firmly to do so. One ghost, Tania, says she once begged an author, a well-known tycoon, to read his biography in the hours before it went to the publisher, because as she quite rightly suspected even though he had the draft for some weeks, he hadn't opened the document, let alone reviewed his book.

'He was a busy man, so I sent it to him some weeks ahead of deadline. I had a few one line emails saying it looked fine but I just sensed he hadn't read it. I was really nervous because I had had to fill in a fair bit of detail and I needed him to sign it off at the very least. Eventually, after a lot of nagging, he reluctantly read it, just hours before the final deadline. He didn't make that many changes to the copy but the handful he did make were pretty significant.'

Although this period is a nerve-wracking time for a ghost, it signals they are close to the end of their involvement in the job. Once the edits have been done and the manuscript approved by the author, their work is pretty much over. The publisher may ask for some additional material, such as copy for the back cover, or an epilogue, or ask the ghost to give the final edit of the manuscript the once over, but other than that, it is over to the author.

Occasionally, the author may ask the ghost to come along to publicity meetings with their publishers, because right then they are the only other person on the planet who knows the material as well as they do. The ghost could prove invaluable in pulling out publicity angles from the manuscript that could be fed into the media. It is, however, the time that the author and their ghost will part company.

Chapter Ten
When things go wrong

At its simplest, any difference between an author and their ghost manifest themselves as a straight, occasionally heated, denial by the named author that they've used a ghost at all. As discussed in chapter one, John F Kennedy, went to his grave denying he'd worked with a ghost on his book Profiles in Courage, which won him a Pulizer Prize for his 'solo' effort in writing it. It wasn't until years later that his speech-writer Ted Sorenson confirmed what everyone suspected when he admitted in the Wall Street Journal he did 'a first draft of most of the chapters' and 'helped choose the words of many of its sentences'.

Kennedy is not the only celebrity to deny the help of a ghost, but curiosity about who did and didn't write a book, fuelled at least in part by public denials like this, have made things awkward for anyone wanting to cast doubt on the existence of ghosts. Ironically, at the same time, they have also made things tougher for people who didn't use one at all. Indeed, the public's apparent fascination for spotting any sign of a co-author, particularly among well-known celebrity works, can mean *any* celebrity should be prepared for an uncomfortable time when they produce a book. In the Spring of 2012 New York Times food writer Julia Moskin got into a very public spat with a number of celebrity cookbook authors, including Gwyneth Paltrow and Rachael Ray. Moskin had written an article claiming that recipes are very often conceived by a team of assistants and, occasionally, famous foodies don't even so much as read the books that bear their name. The celebrity chefs named in the piece adamantly denied the involvement of ghosts in their work but Moskin, who has ghosted nine cookbooks, was unrepentant. As the row rumbled on, she pointed out that it is a fine line between ghost cooking, assistance and collaboration and insisted it is hardly surprising that busy celebrities who had restaurants, brands and media empires to run, call in the experts.

The flipside to this is sometimes ghosts dispute their author's account of their collaborative relationship. One of the most famous examples of this was between Pablo Fenjves the ghostwriter of OJ Simpson's controversial book '*If I did it*'. Fenjves went on the record to vehemently deny the US football star-turned-actor's account of the creation, content and hypothetical description of the slaying of his former wife Nicole Brown Simpson. He said if there were any errors in the controversial book, they were fed to him by Simpson, or the star failed to correct them.

Occasionally, disagreements between a ghost and author go much, much further than a last minute denial of one another's existence. Perhaps the most thorough and publicly acrimonious breakdown of a collaborative agreement in recent years was that between the WikiLeaks founder Julian Assange and his ghost Andrew O'Hagan. Three years after the pair began to work together on a project that publisher Canongate had sold to 40 countries in a $2.5 million deal, the pairing collapsed. O'Hagan subsequently wrote in the London Review of Books that Assange was 'a mercurial character'. In a detailed expose of the relationship he said his co-writer was, by turns, passionate, funny, lazy, courageous, vain, paranoid, moral and manipulative. The ghost concluded quite early on that Assange's book wouldn't work because he felt the man who put himself in charge of disclosing the world's secrets simply couldn't bear his own. In O'Hagan's view, the story of Assange's life mortified the author and that is why he made one excuse after another not to complete the project. Indeed, according to the ghost, Assange didn't want to do the book and hadn't right from the beginning.

In the end, Canongate became so exasperated by Assange's stalling and non co-operation it published a version of O'Hagan's manuscript as '*Julian Assange: The Unauthorised Biography*' in September 2011. It didn't have the author's consent, indeed he publically denounced it, but according to O'Hagan

Assange covertly encouraged sales through social media links to Amazon. It made little difference. Despite its massive advance and publicity, book sales remained stubbornly low.

From a ghosting point of view, the most interesting part of this story is how thoroughly a promising relationship between collaborators can break-down. O'Hagan, an award-winning, Booker nominated novelist in his own right, appeared initially fascinated by the boldness of the WikiLeaks founder, who at the start of the project in January 2011 was living with a group of supporters at Ellingham Hall in Norfolk, while bailed over allegations of rape and sexual assault in Sweden. As the relationship developed, O'Hagan began to become alarmed by his co-writer's growing paranoia and erratic behaviour. In one car journey together Assange became convinced he was being tailed and ordered the writer to pull off the road. The pursuer turned out to be a perfectly innocent taxi, dropping a child off at school. When Assange visited his local police station as part of his bail conditions, he would get his PA to check the bushes for assassins before he went in. The author's very vocal disdain for a large number of former collaborators who he now regarded as 'enemies' should have been a big warning sign to O'Hagan and Canongate and sure enough, Assange's publishers were later added to his personal black list. O'Hagan managed to keep the relationship with Assange amicable, even as the book deal finally collapsed, but later acknowledged his co-author would hate his eventual exposure of the process in the press.

Thankfully cases like this are rare, but they can happen. Most ghosts will tell stories of collaborations that have gone awry and very often it will be because the author is horrified at seeing their story in print. One ghost, Elle gives a typical example.

'I spent a lot of time on a book with a well known business man and he came across as a bit of an arrogant twit. He read the draft and was furious that he came across as an arrogant twit. He threatened to sue everyone and anyone involved in the project. The book got canned in the end and I had to chalk it up to experience.

'This man's problem was not with my writing. He just didn't like looking in the mirror.'

Fortunately the Assange/O'Hagan story is an accelerated and greatly amplified version of what ghosts occasionally go through with some authors. It is, however, worth considering what can be done to help see a project through to a successful conclusion. While it is not always easy to get things back on track once the cracks begin to appear, it is possible with some forward planning and some careful management.

The first, and possibly easiest way, to ward off future disputes is for a ghost to share draft chapters with the author all the way through the process. Indeed, some agencies such as Diane Banks

Associates now insist on this arrangement in their contracts. Diane Banks says:

We had one nasty case a few years ago. The subject decided they didn't want to write the book after all after they saw the copy, which incidentally we thought was excellent.

In the wake of that incident we now insist a ghost is contractually obliged to show the subject the chapters as they go along. We also make sure there are sufficient clauses covering cooperation. Even if it is just an agreement to show the first three chapters to check if it is right and the tone the author is looking for, then there are not going to be any kind of surprises down the line.

A legally binding contract is, of course, one of the most important steps of the whole ghosting process and will, at least in part, mitigate against future problems. Although the basis of a good collaboration is a good degree of trust between the two parties, it always, always makes sense to sort out a solid written agreement right from the off. This way, everyone has something to refer back to should things not work out as expected.

New York-based agent Madeleine Morel says it is the only way to proceed, because you just never know how a project will end.

Authors run the gamut from the ones who treat a ghost writer like a glorified secretary and who barely do anything to advance the book, to those who are such control freaks that they have to approve every

semi colon. You never know where you are going to end up on that spectrum and that is why my contracts are more and more tightly written.

I had a perfect example recently of someone who was signed up to do a book for a business publisher. It was supposed to be a book about a leading computer company, but the named author decided the book should be about her. The ghost knew the editor wanted a business book, but the author insisted that everything had to be pre-approved before it went to the editor. Every time the poor ghost tried to write the book the editor wanted, the author threw it out. This ghost went round and round, producing multiple drafts of the manuscript. After that experience I added a clause in the contract to the effect that the ghostwriter would only have to do one complete rewrite before a book goes to the editor.

To some extent you learn from the mistakes and situations as they present themselves.

Another time a celebrity foodie author was so phobic about their ghost having any contact with the editor that he absolutely wouldn't permit it at all. He was a control freak, even though he was never really involved in the book in the way he should have been either. Of course, the manuscript ended-up a disaster. The ghost, who had tons of New York Times bestsellers under her belt, was tearing her hair out. She was contacting me and saying: could you please ask the publishing editor to contact me? Finally she contacted the editor directly and it was the only way the book got finished.

When we came to the next book deal, this guy who was represented by an attorney, said: let's do the deal and we'll use the same boilerplate contract. I went through the contract, as I always do, to make sure nothing had been snuck in. There in the confidentiality clause, I found a new clause. It said if the ghost abused or contravened the confidentiality clause, in any way, which included contacting the publishing editor, they could be sued for up to a million dollars. The attorney wouldn't move it and he even made out it was a reasonable request. I thought it was ludicrous. Needless to say, we walked away from the deal and I suggested they find another writer.

The role of a contract is to define rights and remedies should everything not work out as expected. And, however agreeable the initial meeting between an author or ghost, sooner or later, the unexpected does generally happen. Fortunately, most relationships grow to be strong enough to withstand the odd bump in the road, but as we have already seen, this isn't always the case.

There are all sorts of things that can happen too. Say a book written in collaboration turned out to be a rip-roaring success, exceeding everyone's original expectations many times over. If there is not a negotiated and well structured fee agreement in place, that sets out everyone's deal in clear terms, there is little in place to stop a ghost 're-interpreting' themselves as an official 'co-author' and claiming a far larger share of the profits than either party intended at the outset. Similarly, without the protection of a contract, what is to prevent an author writing the ghost out of the picture altogether and denying their involvement so they can get every penny of future royalties? As with any creative endeavour, where there is an element of chance whether or not a project will succeed, it may well start out nicely, with both sides doing their best for the overall product. However, success, and indeed failure, can breed a surprising amount of animosity. If everyone is clear on their terms from the start, there will be no cause for disagreement later on.

Many publishers will insist, as a condition of working with an author and ghost team, there is formal written agreement between them. Even if this is not the case, it is highly advisable to get one in place.

So what would a collaborative contract cover? The key points are compensation, ownership and control, credit, responsibilities, dispute resolution, copyright and libel. There may also be a miscellaneous section for items such as media rights, licensing and sequel rights. Let's take each element in turn.

All ghosting contracts should cover *compensation*, which is how much both parties will be paid and whether or not the ghost is due a percentage share of royalties. It will also detail when and how each party will be paid. As detailed earlier, sometimes ghosts are paid in installments, perhaps on agreement that part of the manuscript is signed off and approved before the next installment is paid. Other times ghosts will expect their whole fee paid up-front, or fifty per cent up-front and the rest on delivery. This all needs to be set out in writing and the compensation section should also look at expenses and tie down who will pay if the ghost has to travel widely to conduct interviews and stay away from home. Often, both sides will agree to share expenses, just as they agree to share royalties, but again it is best to discuss this openly.

Another important point to discuss early on is *ownership* and *control*. Who is controlling the project in terms of whose responsibility is it to seek out book deals and who has the authority to approve the final draft of the work, or seek revisions? This is particularly pertinent when there are more than two authors involved. Say a group of entrepreneurs got together with a ghost to write a 'how we did it' inspirational book, it would be very helpful to set out how they would all work together on this creative project. Would they want to be unanimous over every decision on the book's direction, or would a simple majority vote be OK?

Even if it is a straight agreement between one author and their ghost, they should discuss approval rights over the manuscript. This will put an author's mind at rest because it guarantees material will never be shown to any third party, such as a publisher, or agent, until they themselves have seen it and signed it off. This clause is a good thing for a ghost too, because it makes a lot more sense to agree everything up front with an author, before the manuscript is widely circulated. The last thing anyone wants is for a publisher to get excited about new copy, only for an author to subsequently demand huge cuts because he or she didn't get a chance to go through it properly first.

It is very important to get something concrete in place to manage expectations from the beginning. As ghost Douglas Wight found on one project, if everyone assumes something different on ownership and control a project can quickly unravel.

With one project we embarked on the writing before a book deal was in place. Eventually, however, we had an offer and we even had a serialisation set up in the Guardian. However, from the beginning we struggled. The publisher had clear ideas on how the book should be structured even before the contract was signed. Their idea was quite different to what we had laid out in the original proposal. Once we got going there was so much to-ing and fro-ing that the author eventually got cold feet. He just wasn't interested in doing it anymore. It didn't help that the book focused on a dramatic episode for him and going over and over it several times was actually making things worse. Far from being a cathartic experience, the book was making him constantly relive an event in his life he would rather forget. While we were going backwards and forwards arguing over structure, he was getting nightmares. Not surprisingly, the deal collapsed. It was quite frustrating

because we had got to the point where I felt we were close to what everyone wanted, but by then it was irretrievable.

It would not be unreasonable for a ghost to impose a reasonable limitation on the approvals process. They may, for example, ask for at least 30-days after receiving the author's comments to resubmit. There might also be a provision for what constitutes a 'satisfactory' manuscript and it will probably reference the original book proposal ie if the book closely follows the format agreed in the initial plan, it should for all intents and purposed be deemed satisfactory. This protects both parties in case either one of them tries to move the goal posts during the process, contrary to the other collaborator's wishes.

The contract stage is also the time where an author and their ghost need to agree on what *credit* the co-writer will get, if at all and if they do get one, how prominent it will be. Opinions vary wildly over how much, or how little, credit a ghost should get and where on the book their name should be included. Neil Simpson, for example, says he never expects, or seeks credit.

I am happy for my name not to appear at all. I have never been bothered about it. My feeling is that as long as the publisher knows who did it and so does my agent and any one else that is important in the industry, that is fine. They are the people who will get me my next job. I don't need Mr and Mrs Bloggs who bought the book in WH Smiths to know.

There are many ghosts who will push hard to get some form of recognition, so they can use their involvement in the project as a foot in the door to get other jobs. Other ghosts will also argue that occasionally the level of involvement will warrant a decent credit. The key is to remain flexible, says Tim Tate.

When I wrote *Slave Girl* with Sarah Forsyth I felt I deserved a credit. I sat down with her and recorded many hours of material, which took a lot of sorting and shifting. I also had to do many hours of research outside of this, interviewing friends, family and the police that handled her case. It wasn't a case of sitting down with a tape recorder, they say something and I write it down.

Another time I collaborated on a book where I was given a 180,000 word manuscript and asked to cut it down to 80,000 words. I didn't seek a credit and wasn't offered one. It really depends on the project.

Even if a ghost does feel he or she warrants recognition in some form, the prominence of this credit is something they may have to work hard to negotiate for. While some authors will agree to a joint credit on the cover, most publishers are very reluctant indeed to give such prominence to a ghost. Indeed, some publishers say they will actively discourage authors from using a particular ghost, if the ghost insists on overt credit. Very often, the best a ghost will be able to secure is a mention in the acknowledgment section. It is up to an individual ghost to decide whether this is sufficient recognition, or if they would rather work elsewhere.

This is not to say all ghosts will push for a credit, or indeed battle for any public acknowledgement at all. Indeed, some actively shun any public mention whatsoever. Rebecca Farnworth, who ghosted three volumes of Katie Price's bestselling autobiography, is also said to be the author of the model and reality TV star's two novels, *Angel* and *Crystal*. However, the ghost has never spoken publicly to confirm or deny this fact. Ghostly detectives may note that Farnworth's credit appears on the copyright page of the two fictional books, but she isn't telling, turning down all requests for interviews. Her stance makes a lot of sense. Price is the celebrity that drives the sales of her books and the draw that gets publishers commissioning further ones. In instances like this, it doesn't make any sense for a ghost who is unknown outside of the industry to pop up and claim the credit. While there is a healthy scepticism among Price's fans, based on whether or not she has penned the books, it is not enough to put them off queuing to buy them. If her ghost is willing to fade into the background, it works perfectly for all concerned.

Where things can go very wrong is when an agreement has been struck about credit between the ghost and author and is written in black and white into the contract, then at the eleventh hour the author tries to renegotiate the terms of the deal. This has been known to happen once the manuscript is submitted, or even just as the project is about to go to print.

As Lynne Barrett-Lee explains, being cast off and denied after all the hard work that goes into writing a book, is a frustrating experience for a ghost.

There have been situations where people have said yes, yes, yes, all the way through, but when the process nears the end they try to renegotiate terms. Once the book starts coming together – all those words, all those chapters – it's easy to think that it all looks so easy and start to lose sight of the fact that the book wouldn't be there at all if it wasn't for the skill of their ghost. That is the blessing and the curse of the ghostwriter. If you are good, when you come out of the other end of the process, the person that you've ghosted for thinks they could probably have done it themselves.

I totally understand that – hindsight is a wonderful thing, and perhaps it's human nature. Thankfully, though, it's rare. In my experience, anyway. But it's also why ghostwriters need contracts.

The next item on the list is *responsibilities*. This is where both parties are as specific as possible about what is to be delivered and when. This section may even be as specific as setting out a few timelines along the way, such as how quickly a first draft might be available. Deadlines are, of course, critical in publishing. A missed deadline can cause havoc and even the cancellation of a book contract. In this scenario, it could trigger an obligation for the writing team to pay back any advance, which is something no one wants to happen.

It is very useful from a ghost's point of view to insert some detail into the contract about what will be expected from the author. While the onus is very much on the co-writer to come up with the goods, it is worth making it clear right from the start what an author brings to the party. It is generally more than their name. For a collaboration to work, an author has to commit to X number of hours of interviews with their ghost. The amount can vary from writer to writer, but if both parties agree up front on at least roughly the number of hours needed, there will be no surprises later on.

Likewise, an author may like a clause on confidentiality, because authors have to feel comfortable that anything they tell their ghost will remain between the two parties until it is approved for publication. Indeed, some well known figures will insist on a confidentiality agreement before they even speak to prospective ghosts, although this isn't altogether necessary because it would be pretty daft for any professional ghost to sully their reputation by dashing off to the tabloids with every bit of gossip they gleaned.

Although no one likes to talk about what happens if things go wrong, the contract should address what might happen if it does. What are the procedures for *dispute resolution*? What are the steps that both parties should take if they feel unhappy or uncomfortable with the progress on the book?

As with most things in the corporate world, a successful collaboration, or at least a successful dispute resolution, comes down to agreeing strong contract terms across the board at the outset. If the contract is solid, both sides should at least be able to walk away relatively unscathed, even if they are hurt by the experience and it leaves long-lasting sensation of being let down.

In January 2014, sports writer Paul Kimmage parted company with Irish rugby legend Brian O'Driscoll. He had been ghosting his biography, but quit the project in a dispute with the author over his decision to give an interview to one paper, ahead of the one he worked for. He had asked O'Driscoll especially to work with his paper on the feature, but the author was unwilling to make the concession. After agreeing to go their separate ways, Kimmage said at the time he had endured a lot of pain over the episode, because a 'loving relationship' had come to an end.

In this case the publisher Penguin stepped in and negotiated an amicable settlement and, as occasionally happens following a dispute between a ghost and an author, another writer had to be found to begin the process again.

Two of the biggest points to consider at this stage are *copyright* and *libel.* Let's take copyright first. Under copyright law, the creator of the work is the copyright owner. If the ghost and author agree to share the copyright that is fine, however, if the intention is for the ghost to assign the full copyright over to the author, this has to be done in writing and a provision to this effect must be included in the contract. Copyrights cannot be transferred verbally.

Libel is a much less clear-cut subject and without care can be a real danger for everyone involved in writing a book. By definition, libel is an untrue statement about a person, published in writing, or through broadcast media. Whoever writes and publishes a defamatory statement is held liable, which means a ghost is just as much in the frame as the author themselves if something untrue finds its way into the manuscript. This can present a bit of a quandary to a ghost writer. Although they will endeavor to check and re-check every fact, they are, to some extent in their author's hands. Say an author describes a controversial conversation they've had with one other party. No one else was in the room, but the material discussed was pretty explosive stuff. The author may swear blind they said this or that and the other person answered in a particular way. As the ghost was not in the room, facts like this are almost impossible to check. On the one hand the ghost won't want to be liable for a lawsuit, yet on the other, if the conversation is central to the theme of the book and sheds some important light on the main narrative, they may be keen to see it included.

The only answer is to ensure there is a strong clause in the contract that indemnifies a ghost should anything they write turn out to be libelous. By the same token, there also needs to be a reciprocal clause which protects the author, should a ghost go off at a tangent and add some detail which later turns out to get them both into trouble.

In the final, or *miscellaneous* part, the author and ghost should consider licensing and alternative media rights should the book be sold to be made into a film or TV series. Who will benefit from further deals like this and if there is to be a continuing relationship, who gets what? Plus, regarding that future relationship, would the author like to give the ghost first refusal on any further projects he or she has planned?

Another miscellaneous item is to ensure everyone holds on to any material, such as recorded interviews, books, notes, transcripts and research material used in the writing of the book. This is essential in case there are any legal disputes once it is published.

Sorting out detail on contracts at the beginning of a collaboration may feel like it puts a bit of a dampener on what should be the start of an exciting creative endeavor. Some of the more circumspect among the ghosting community may say they are happy enough to get paid to do their job and move on, while authors may be simply champing at the bit to get their story on the page. However, contracts are a necessary because it doesn't always end as people expect. This is when lawyers start sharpening their pencils, or when very public spats begin in the media and no one wants to be at the business end of that sort of attention.

Ghosts always expect their role to diminish hugely once the writing is done. It is all part of subsuming their ego, which is what they sign up for in this business. They may even have to supress a slight giggle when they see their author telling chat show hosts how hard to was to knuckle down and write their book. The last thing they want though is to become part of the 'publicity' around a book, as they and the author argue about the end product. Hopefully, once the contract is signed, neither party will ever look at it again. However, if there is one in place, it will stop a great deal of heartache later on.

CONCLUSIONS

For many years, ghostwriting used to be the publishing world's guilty little secret. Indeed, the name itself illustrates a desire for secrecy, anonymity and invisibility. Yet, while ghosts are happy to stay in the background, the profession is seeing a subtle shift. Not only do more people believe in ghosts, they are happy to accept they are all around us and an acceptable, indeed essential, part of the publishing mix. Some publishers are even prepared to market the signing of an established ghost as a coup for a particular writer. Having a good ghost is a mark of prestige and proof a book will be a decent quality.

This acceptance of the reality of ghosts is signalled by the gradual re-naming of the profession. Ghosts are more frequently referred to as collaborators, or co-authors and even occasionally grace the front page credits, rather than haunting the depths of the acknowledgement section.

This doesn't mean ghosts can kid themselves they have any more ownership over a title than they ever had and supressing their ego is still an essential part of the business. It does, however, mean ghosts can enjoy the freedom and variety of a fantastic job and can, just occasionally, step out of the shadows.

Ghostwriting is, without a doubt, one of the richest and varied careers there is. There are few jobs where there is the opportunity to ask a famous person absolutely anything, however personal, or to be in at the beginning of the breaking of a most extraordinary story from a supposedly ordinary person. Similarly, there are few careers which offer such a rich variety of experiences. From one book to the next, a ghostwriter may find themselves being flown on a private jet to an elite private soiree, to hanging around while their subject delivers a calf before they can finish an interview, to being given carte blanche to rummage through the drawers and cupboards of a film legend.

Ghosts have to be experts at reading their subject's moods, adapting to their foibles and grabbing every moment possible in their often impossible schedules in order to get the copy they need. It's not always easy. Indeed, one ghost relates how she only got her subject to finally give her the time she needed for interviews when he was jailed for a diamond robbery. Sometimes a ghost just has to take the only break they can.

They also need to pull off a careful balancing act. When working with an author they frequently juggle the role of friend, counsellor and wordsmith, yet quite often they will have to push their subject hard to get the copy needed for a commercial product. Meanwhile, this close relationship may also present a personal challenge to ghostwriters. Ghosts are often called-upon to pen some quite harrowing stories and have no option but to fully immerse themselves in the content. Writers need to use various techniques to set their own boundaries and protect themselves.

It is in the nature of the job that ghosts build up close relationships with their subjects, but it is a fleeting, even impersonal, relationship. William Novak assumed he would be like Lee Iacocca's 'surrogate son', when he was chosen to write the memoir of the US tycoon. It was Novak's first ghosting project and he quickly found that this wasn't the case and indeed never is. Yes, the 50 hours or so of interviews between the two men were intense, but the relationship was business-like and ruthlessly efficient. If any ghost is ever in doubt that this is way of the world, the proof is always there at the end of a project. When it is over, it is over. Once a manuscript is produced and approved, it is more than likely the collaborators may never even speak to one another again.

It is a situation ghosts learn to get used to. Rather like a very intense holiday romance which is doomed to end because the protagonists live on different sides of the world, a ghost and author are never destined to have a long-term relationship. As one ghost who has worked with a number of celebrity clients says, it is unsettling the first few times, but over time it is possible to accept.

'To begin with I thought this is marvellous, I have made a friend of such and such. Then you realise you are not their friend. I do remember saying at the end of a project with one well known person; oh well, we'll be in touch. She said; I don't think we will, but I will remember you fondly. I thought, actually, that is exactly as it should be. We are not going to be friends. Why would we be? We live in different worlds.'

Clare who ghosted the biography for an A list actress described in chapter eight, said when they parted company she was bereft. It taught her a big lesson.

'The woman was a huge hero of mine. It was such an intense process that afterwards I realised I had fallen in love with her. Famous and successful people are incredibly persuasive, which is why they are famous and successful. I had reached the stage where I would have done anything for her and became possessed with the idea of getting the book finished for her.

'Afterwards, there was this huge sense of loss. The praise started appearing for the book, but she had done this huge vanishing act from my life. It was like a break-up. I clearly remember driving somewhere in my car and feeling this huge sense of rejection. I couldn't understand why I felt this way and said to myself; it is only a job!

'I saw her a while later and it was lovely but it was like closing a door. Previously I had felt like we had spent our deepest, darkest, most intimate moments together, but when we met again I realised she didn't know a thing about me. She couldn't even remember the names of my children. I had just been another member of her audience.

'A ghost can't get too involved. We're prostitutes, literary hookers. I am fine with that now.'

Ghosts can't even count on the fact they'll be invited to the book launch. Even if an author has been prepared to give their ghost a prominent billing, or even a significant nod in their direction in the acknowledgements, few people are really ready to share the limelight at the book launch. Once again, that is how it should be. It is the way the relationship works. A ghost brings their writing skills to a project, while the author is the name that sells the books. Often, during the writing process, ghosts will become so involved in the story, they may begin to convince themselves it is 'their' book, but at the end of the day it isn't and most writers get that.

No ghost should be lured to the profession by the promise of fame. Fortune maybe, if they are good, but never fame. Ghosts have to have no ego, be invisible and most importantly, happy to stay that way. If supressing the need for recognition is ever a problem, they can always remember they have huge control. A ghost is the person who will structure a story, decide what to include and exclude and how to bring it alive. That is quite a powerful position to be in.

As for that fortune, the rewards can be considerable for anyone with talent who is prepared to check their ego at the door. However, the amount a ghost is able to earn can and does vary wildly, even for a single individual on a project-by-project basis. Deals are cut in a number of ways, from a split of profits, to straight fee-based agreements, to a spiralling rate of fees. There is often a tussle between celebrities, ghosts and their respective agents over who gets what. Well-known ghosts, with a respected track record, are in a good position to negotiate and some big name celebrity autobiographies can earn them six figure advances.

Upheavals in modern publishing mean working practices and commercial arrangements are constantly changing for ghosts and the industry itself has had to adapt. Professional writers can sometimes be persuaded to take a leap of faith over projects they take on and produce detailed book proposals on spec. Most are understandably choosy about investing their time in this way, but know that if they get it right they may well be rewarded with a share of an international bestseller.

The potential fees on offer for ghosting have attracted a growing number of established authors to explore the profession in recent years. Previously, established writers were slightly sneering about ghosts, even assuming it is not 'proper' authorship.

Yet, today literary agents report a rise in authors who have already published under their own name seeking ghosting collaborations. It is an obvious choice of career for anyone struggling to secure decent advances with their literary novels. Ghosting, at least from a writing career point of view, has apparently come in from the cold.

Of course, from a publishing view-point, ghosts have long been welcomed. Putting interesting, possibly famous, people together with talented storytellers to produce a commercially viable product makes perfect business sense, so why wouldn't a publisher appreciate a good ghost? There are an awful lot of people with intriguing stories, or who appeal to the public because of their fame/knowledge/style/talent (delete as applicable), yet very often these people are either incapable of writing, or don't have the time. Cynically pushing out any old rubbish in the hope a celebrities name will sell it won't work. The book will quickly run out of steam. The only way to give a book a chance of working well in a crowded market is to bring in a professional.

Successful author/ghost collaborations will always lead to more work too. Publishers who have a hit with a partnership often cast around to find other ways to benefit from the market and this could well extend a franchise from non fiction into fiction titles and even children's books.

Meanwhile, although the media and some commentators like to play spot-the ghost and occasionally try to snobbishly whip up some controversy over the fact a public figure has 'shock' 'horror' not written their own book, few outside the publishing industry know or care about whether an author has had help. Most readers are mainly interested in whether the book they've bought is a good read and the fact it accurately reflects their view of the personality of the person whose name is on the cover is a bonus. The rest is just detail. We are, after all, obsessed with celebrity and fame today and ghostwriting is just one of many legitimate ways to feed the hunger for more information about people in the public eye.

Not every ghosting collaboration will be a runaway success for a variety of reasons. Sometimes, people are convinced they have a fantastic story to tell, but in reality they only have the making of one or two good chapters in them. Other times authors are so shocked by the reality of seeing their story laid out in front of them on the printed page, they can hardly bear it. In most instances though, problems like this can be foreseen and ironed out, well before the first word is typed. Even so, projects do occasionally fail and it can be devastating for all concerned.

Happily, by far the majority of ghosting partnerships are a success. The author ends up with the book they always wanted to write and their ghost has the satisfaction of making a decent living out of doing an extraordinary job.

Appendix

Who's who

Many of the contributors to this book have spoken anonymously, however some have generously agreed to be named and brief biographies follow:

Diane Banks

Diane Banks founded Diane Banks Associates, a literary and talent agency based in central London representing commercial fiction and personality-led, media or current affairs based non-fiction, in 2006 following 10 years in London's trade publishing houses including Penguin and Hodder & Stoughton. Diane sat on the committee of the Association of Authors' Agents 2012 – 2015.

Lynne Barrett-Lee

Lynne Barrett-Lee is the author of eight novels, including her acclaimed debut, *Julia Gets a Life,* and *Barefoot in the Dark,* which was shortlisted for the 2007 Melissa Nathan Award for Comedy Romance. Her novels have been translated into several languages and she has also contributed two titles (one ghostwritten for GMTV's Fiona Phillips) to the UK's Quick Reads Campaign, which provides easy-to-read books for adult emergent readers.

Lynne's ghostwriting career began in 2007, when she was approached by a former patient of her Oncologist husband, to ask if she would help her write the story of her amazing life. The result was the 2009 title *Never Say Die*. Since then, Lynne has collaborated on a wide range of titles in several different genres.

Ingrid Connell

Ingrid Connell is a non fiction editorial director at Pan Macmillan, publishing on the Sidgwick & Jackson and Pan lists. The majority of books she publishes are autobiographies, from celebrities to inspirational memoirs. Her bestselling titles include Lord Sugar's autobiography *What You See is What You Get*, Coleen Nolan's *Upfront and Personal* Amanda Owen's *The Yorkshire Shepherdess* and *My Secret Sister* by Helen Edwards and Jenny Lee Smith.

Deborah Crewe

Deborah Crewe grew up in Colchester, Essex. She studied at Oxford, Harvard and London Business School and was, until recently, a senior civil servant. Since she turned to ghostwriting three years ago, Deborah has been involved in writing projects across a range of genres, including *Coming Up Trumps*, the Sunday Times bestselling memoir by

TEENA LYONS

the indomitable Lady Trumpington; *Call the Vet*, a memoir of a country vet's first year in practice; *Jail Bird: The Life and Crimes of an Essex Bad Girl*, the ultimately inspiring story of a drug-dealer turned pig farmer and *Last Man Standing: Memoirs of a Political Survivor*, the memoirs of former Foreign Secretary, Home Secretary and Lord Chancellor Jack Straw.

Andrew Crofts

Andrew Crofts is a ghostwriter and author who has published more than eighty books, a dozen of which were Sunday Times number one bestsellers. He has also guided a number of international clients successfully through the minefield of independent publishing.

He has also published his own fiction, most recently "*Secrets of the Italian Gardener*", which draws on his experience amongst the powerful and wealthy.

His books on writing include "*Ghostwriting*", (A&C Black) and "*The Freelance Writer's Handbook*", (Piatkus), which has been reprinted eight times over twenty years and "*Confessions of a Ghostwriter*" (Friday Project).

Louise Dixon

Louise Dixon has worked for several publishing houses on non-fiction titles ranging from biography, history and language to highly illustrated general reference works. She has been an editorial director at Michael O'Mara books Limited since 2007.

Trevor Dolby

Trevor Dolby has worked in publishing for more than 30 years, starting out writing and researching commissioned books for Michael Joseph. He has worked for John Murray as Science Editor, been Natural History Editor at Reed and Publishing Director at Pavillion. In the mid 90s, Trevor set up the non-fiction list at Orion which went on to become one of the most successful imprints of the early 2000s, winning the Editor and Imprint of the Year award at the 2003 British Book Awards. In 2007 he set up Preface with Rosie de Courcy under the umbrella of Random House which publishes a diverse list of fiction and non-fiction.

Nadene Ghouri

Nadene Ghouri is a former correspondent of both the BBC and Al Jazeera English, who has reported from places as diverse as Afghanistan, Democratic Republic of Congo, Iran, Lebanon and Pakistan. She is the co-author of two best selling books *The Favored Daughter - One woman's fight to lead Afghanistan into the future with Fawzia Koof* (Pan Macmillan) and *Born Into The Children of God - my struggle to escape a religious sex cult* with Natacha Tormey (Harper Collins 2014). She is currently writing her first novel.

Caro Handley

Caro Handley graduated from York University with a degree in politics and philosophy and specialised in

African politics, having grown up in Kenya. Before moving into publishing she worked as a journalist. She trained on local newspapers in South Wales and Peterborough before moving into magazines and the national press, working for Woman Magazine as a feature writer, The Daily Mail as a reporter, Woman's Own as Assistant Editor and The Sunday Express Magazine as Assistant Editor where she ghosted a column for a rising young star, Jonathan Ross. She then went freelance and worked for a wide variety of magazines over the next ten years, including stints as agony aunt for Chat magazine and later for Good Housekeeping.

Caro, who is also trained as a counsellor/psychotherapist has published 7 books under her own name and ghosted 33 more since 1999.

Natalie Jerome

Having previously worked at Ebury, Macmillan and Virgin Books, Natalie joined HarperCollins seven years ago and is Publisher of HarperNonFiction. She has acquired and edited some of entertainment's biggest names, including Alan Carr, Chris Evans, One Direction and new global sensation 5 Seconds of Summer. Natalie also champions the Creative Access programme, which promotes representation of young people from under-represented backgrounds within publishing and across the media.

Shannon Kyle

Shannon Kyle is a Sunday Times best selling ghostwriter and to date she has written ten books, covering genres including celebrity, historical and misery memoirs. Before she was a ghost writer, Shannon started her career on a local newspaper and was short listed for Young Journalist of the year in 2001. She went on to work as a national newspaper journalist for The Sunday People, and she has also written for the Guardian, Mirror, The Sun and specialises in real life stories for the women's consumer weekly market.

David Long

Aside from three years spent working as a magazine editor, David Long has been a freelance writer since graduating in 1983. A regular contributor to The Times, Sunday Times and Sunday People, he ghosted for several British and US publishers before the first of more than twenty books appeared under his own name in 2006. His first book for children was published in 2014.

Andrew Lownie

After a period as a bookseller and journalist, Andrew began his publishing career as a graduate trainee at Hodder & Stoughton. In 1985 he became an agent at John Farquharson, now part of Curtis Brown, and the following year became the youngest director in British publishing when he was appointed a director. He is also an author in his own right, most notably of a biography of John Buchan and a literary companion to Edinburgh. He founded the Andrew Lownie Literary Agency in 1988 and it is now one of the UK's leading boutique literary agencies.

Madeleine Morrel

Madeleine Morrel has had a life long career in publishing. In 1982, she established 2M Communications, a literary agency specialising in non-fiction titles. Working extensively with both established and first-time authors she has sold hundreds of book projects. In recent years, Madeleine has established herself as a literary matchmaker using her professional and intuitive instinct to put together writers, authors, agents and publishing editors.

Emma Murray

Emma Murray is a ghostwriter and author, specialising in business, academic, and psychology books. She is the author of *The Unauthorized Guide to Doing Business the Alan Sugar Way* (Wiley-Capstone 2010), *How to Succeed as a Freelancer in Publishing* (How To Books 2010), and co-author of academic textbook *Organizational Behavior* (Wiley US 2015). She lives in London, with her husband and two young children.

Katharine Quarmby

Katharine Quarmby is a contributing editor at *Newsweek Europe* and award-winning writer, journalist and film-maker specialising in social affairs with an investigative edge. She has has made many films for the BBC, as well as working as a correspondent for the *Economist*, an associate editor for Prospect magazine and contributing to British broadsheets, including the *Guardian, Sunday Times* and the *Telegraph*.

Her first book for adults, about her investigations, *Scapegoat: why we are failing disabled people* (Portobello Press, 2011), won a prestigious international award, the Ability Media Literature award, in 2011. Her second non-fiction book, on Gypsies, Roma and Travellers in the UK, *No Place to Call Home: Inside the Real Lives of Gypsies and Travellers*, was published by Oneworld in 2013 was shortlisted for the Bread and Roses Non-Fiction award. She also enjoys writing books and short plays for young children, with her first book, *Fussy Freya*, published in 2008, and a school play, *Rosy Gets The Plot*, touring in 2014 with the Little Angel Puppet Theatre.

Alan Samson

Alan Samson is Publisher of Non-Fiction for the Weidenfeld & Nicolson and Orion lists. He joined Orion in 2003 after 12 years as an Editorial Director at Little, Brown. His list of non-fiction authors includes Antonia Fraser, Antony Beevor, Julie Walters, Helen Mirren, Sean Connery, A.A. Gill, Catherine Deneuve, Danny Baker, Christopher Meyer, Carol Drinkwater, George Soros and Keith Richards. He has also published books by David Hockney, R.D. Laing, Spike

Milligan, Mitch Albom *Tuesdays With Morrie,* John McEnroe *Serious,* Edwina Currie's Diaries, Malcolm Gladwell's *The Tipping Point* and Roy Keane and Roddy Doyle's *The Second Half.*

Neil Simpson

Neil Simpson has been a staff reporter and section editor on titles as diverse as the Daily Mirror, the Sunday Telegraph and the Mail on Sunday. He began writing celebrity biographies in 2003 and ghosted his first autobiography two years later. He has since made the Sunday Times Top Ten, had books translated into several languages and has sold the TV rights to some books in the UK, Germany, Italy and Australia.

Nicola Stow

Nicola Stow has been a journalist since 2000 and has worked for several national UK newspapers, including the News of the World. She now works as a ghostwriter and freelance journalist. Her books include Born Gangster and Cabin Fever: The Sizzling Secrets of a Virgin Air Hostess. She lives in Edinburgh with her husband.

Tim Tate

Tim Tate is a multiple award-winning documentary film-maker and bestselling author.

He was founder member of ITV's popular and influential Cook Report team and subsequently spent nearly 10 years as producer-director in Yorkshire

Television's acclaimed documentaries department making films for series as diverse as First Tuesday, Network First, Dispatches and Secret History. He is the author of eleven published non-fiction books and runs his own independent production company, Interesting Films.

Jonathan Taylor

Jonathan Taylor has published non-fiction books for nearly 25 years. He has worked for A&C Black, Virgin Books, Trinity Mirror and HarperCollins, and is currently Publishing Director for non-fiction at Headline, part of Hachette UK.

Caroline Upcher

Caroline Upcher worked in story development and production in the film industry, and as a journalist contributing to Conde Nast publications and several national newspapers before her twenty-five year career as an editor of fiction in London and New York publishing. She now runs First Base, an editorial service for first time novelists. She has also written fourteen books, including several crime novels under the name Hope McIntyre featuring a ghostwriter turned detective called Lee Bartholomew.

Tom Watt

Tom Watt is probably best known in the UK as an actor after starring in BBC TV's EastEnders for the first three years of the popular soap opera's run.

Since the late 1980s, he has appeared in West End hits, national tours – including an acclaimed one-man show based on Nick Hornby's Fever Pitch - and several television series. His film credits include And A Nightingale Sang, Patriot Games, Lost Dogs, Flirting With Flamenco, Sherlock Holmes and Small Island.

Tom has also written and broadcast on football for the past fifteen years. His first three books were *The End*, an oral history of Arsenal's famous North Bank terrace; *A Passion For The Game*, 90 first-person accounts of life behind the scenes in the professional game; and *The Greatest Stage*, the official history of Wembley Stadium. He ghost-wrote David Beckham's million-selling autobiography *My Side*.

Katy Weitz

After a decade as a national newspaper feature writer and editor, Katy Weitz founded a real life story agency in 2005. Through First Features she wrote and sold stories to all parts of the national and international media. She ghostwrote her first book *Daddy's Little Secret* in 2010, which has since gone on to sell over 70,000 copies. Her second memoir *Mummy is a Killer* was released in November 2012 and translated into French. She also ghosted *Cellar Girl*, published by Ebury, *Little Drifters*, for HarperCollins and *The Devil On The Doorstep* for Simon & Schuster.

Douglas Wight

Douglas Wight is a former reporter for *the Sun* newspaper, he has held news editor and features editor positions for the *News of the World* and for the last three years before its closure was the paper's Books Editor and a celebrity interviewer. He is the author, ghost or co-writer of seven books, including *Unforgiveable* by Collette Elliott (*Penguin*, 2014), which became a Sunday Times top ten bestseller. He was also the co-writer with actress Emily Lloyd on her memoir *Wish I was there* (*John Blake*, 2013), which the *Mail on Sunday* called the celebrity autobiography of the year.

Printed in Great Britain
by Amazon.co.uk, Ltd.,
Marston Gate.